ANTONIO STRADIVARI

THE CELEBRATED VIOLIN MAKER

Preceded by the Origin and Transformation of Bow Instruments and Followed by a Theoretical Analysis of the Bow

FRANÇOIS-JOSEPH FÉTIS

New Introduction by Stewart Pollens

Dover Publications, Inc.
Mineola, New York

Copyright
Introduction copyright © 2013 by Stewart Pollens.
All rights reserved.

Bibliographical Note

This Dover edition, first published in 2013, is an unabridged republication of *Notice of Anthony Stradivari, the Celebrated Violin-Maker,* originally published by Robert Cocks and Co., London, in 1864. Stewart Pollens has prepared a new Introduction for this Dover edition.

International Standard Book Number
ISBN-13: 978-0-486-49826-3
ISBN-10: 0-486-49826-3

Manufactured in the United States by Courier Corporation
49826301
www.doverpublications.com

FAC SIMILE OF A LETTER WRITTEN BY ANTHONY STRADIVARI.

TO

CHARLES H. C. PLOWDEN, ESQ. F.S.A. F.R.G.S.

AN ARDENT ADMIRER AND COLLECTOR

OF

OLD CREMONESE INSTRUMENTS,

THIS TRANSLATION

IS DEDICATED

BY

THE EDITOR.

INTRODUCTION TO THE DOVER EDITION

FRANÇOIS-Joseph Fétis, the author of *Anthony Stradivari, the Celebrated Violin Maker,* was born in Liège, Belgium in 1784 and died in Brussels in 1871. He began his musical education with his father, Antoine, who was a church organist, violinist, and conductor, and from him François-Joseph learned to play the organ, piano, and violin. At the age of nine he wrote a violin concerto, and by the time he entered the Paris Conservatory in the year 1800 he had composed two piano concertos and three string quartets. At the Paris Conservatory he studied theory and music history, and won a second prize in composition in 1807. He married in 1806 and left Paris with his wife in 1811, settling first in Bouvignes and later Douai, where he taught and worked as a church organist. In 1818 he returned to Paris where he continued teaching and composing (his works include seven comic and dramatic operas, a sacred mass and secular cantata, chamber music, and solo works for piano and organ). In 1821 he received a teaching appointment at the Paris Conservatory and also worked as its librarian from 1826 through 1830. In 1827 Fétis founded the musicological journal *Revue musicale*.

In 1833 he returned to his native Belgium to become the director of the Brussels Conservatory. In addition to his administrative duties, he continued to contribute articles and reviews to newspapers and musical journals, and he wrote numerous methods, treatises, and manuals devoted to harmony, counterpoint, solfège, accompaniment, and composition. Perhaps his most ambitious undertaking was his *Biographie universelle des musiciens et bibliographie générale de la musique*, a multi-volume work published between 1835 and 1844. This comprehensive musical encyclopedia went through numerous editions; the last, published in 1878–1880, was reprinted as recently as 1963. Though Fétis' *Biographie universelle* has come under criticism for factual errors, it remains an invaluable reference work, particularly with regard to events he witnessed and historical figures he knew personally.

Several of Fétis' articles in his *Biographie universelle* were later adapted for republication as monographs. This monograph on Stradivari was first published in Paris in 1856 by the noted violin maker and dealer Jean Baptiste Vuillaume under the title *Antoine Stradivari luthier célèbre connu sous le nom de Stradivarius, précédé de recherches historiques et critiques sur l'origine et les transformations des instruments a archet et suivi d'analyses théoriques sur l'archet et sur François Tourte auteur de ses derniers perfectionnements*. This Dover edition is a reprint of the

English edition published in London by Robert Cocks and Co. in 1864. In addition to the monograph devoted to Stradivari, it includes essays on the origin of bowed instruments, the schools of violin making, the Guarneri family, François-Xavier Tourte, and a technical study of his bows.

Fétis' monograph on Stradivari was translated and edited by John Bishop with the permission of the author. Both Fétis and Bishop acknowledge the technical assistance provided by the violin maker Jean-Baptiste Vuillaume (1798–1875), who began his career in Mirecourt (a French town in the Vosges region largely devoted to violin making) under the tutelage of his father, Claude François. In 1818 Jean-Baptiste moved to Paris to work for the violin maker François Chanot and later for Nicolas-Antoine Lété. In 1825 he set up his own establishment at 46 rue Croix-des-Petits-Champs behind the Louvre and came to dominate the violin trade in the mid-nineteenth century, both as a craftsman and dealer. Vuillaume became one of France's finest violin makers and focused his attention on copying the work of Antonio Stradivari and Giuseppe Guarneri del Gesù. He was said to have had an excellent eye for old instruments, and with his professional interest in the construction of violins and bows, he was clearly the ideal consultant for Fétis.

Fétis begins this work with an essay "Historical Researches on the Origin and Transformations of Bow-Instruments." In this essay, he reconsiders an earlier theory (presented in his "Sketch on the History of the Violin" that appeared in an earlier monograph on Paganini) that the use of a bow with a stringed instrument was an invention of the West, suggesting instead that the Sri Lankan *ravanastron* was the earliest form of bowed instrument, and that it had been invented some fivethousand years before the Christian Era. Most modern historians, however, dispute this and trace bowing back to tenth-century central Asia. Fétis goes on to describe various European precursors of the violin dating from the sixth through the eleventh centuries, such as the *crouth*, *rotta*, *rebec*, and *vielle*, citing textual and iconographic sources and including copious bibliographic references.

Regarding the development of the violin, Fétis drew upon Martin Agricola's *Musica instrumentalis deudsch* (1529), Giovanni Maria Lanfranco's *Scintille di Musica* (1533), Sylvestro Ganassi's *Regola Rubertina* (1542), Scipione Cerreto's *Della prattica musica* (1601), Michael Praetorius's *Syntagma musica* (1619), and Marin Mersenne's *Harmonie universelle* (1636), which remain the principal sources for reconstructing the early history of the violin. (Readers are advised to consult the originals or facsimiles to verify technical details—for example Fétis inaccurately transcribes the tunings of a quartet of viols described in Agricola's Musica *instrumentalis deudsch*.)

Regarding the earliest known violin, Fétis cites Jean-Benjamin de La Borde's *Essay sur la Musique* (Paris, 1780), which describes a four-string violin labeled "Joann. Kerlino, ann. 1449." Fétis remarks that this instrument found its way to Paris and in 1804 came into the hands of the violin maker Jean Gabriel Koliker (active in Paris, 1783–1820). Today, Kerlino is believed to have been a fictional character and the instrument in question either a fabrication by Koliker or perhaps a conversion from an earlier form, such as a viol or lira. The next maker Fétis mentions is Pietro Dardelli of Mantua, and though no violins of his are known today, this Franciscan friar is believed to have made lutes. Fétis then touches upon the work of the Gaspard Duiffoprugcar (also spelled Tieffenbrucker), Ventura Linarolo, Peregrino Zanetto, and one Morglato Morella of Mantua, who supposedly worked in Venice after 1550. Though there is evidence that the first three makers existed, Morglato Morella is apparently another fictional figure whose name has been copied from one biographical dictionary to the next.

Fétis attributes the final form of the violin to the makers Gasparo da Salo, Giovanni Paolo Maggini, and Andrea Amati. In his earlier Paganini monograph, Fétis' states that Andrea Amati was assisted by a brother named Nicolò, yet this brother is not mentioned in the historical essay that accompanies the Stradivari monograph, and recent research has failed to uncover any archival evidence that Andrea had a brother named Nicolò. Fétis states that no birth or death records have been discovered for Andrea Amati. He speculates that Andrea was born sometime during the first two decades of the sixteenth century and that he died around 1580, though later researchers believe that he was born between 1500 and 1505, and it is now known that he died in 1577. Fétis mentions a three-string violin of Andrea's dated 1546 in the collection of Count Cozio de Salabue. Unfortunately, the whereabouts of that violin and an even earlier three-string violin dated 1542 are unknown today. Fétis gives the birth and death dates for Andrea's son Antonio ("Anthony" in this English version) as circa 1550 and 1635, though the dates 1537 and

1607 have been established. Fétis' dates for Antonio's brother Girolamo (otherwise known as Hieronymus, and referred to here as "Jerome") are circa 1550 and 1638, though 1561 has been proposed as his birth year on the basis of a recently discovered document, and modern biographical dictionaries indicate that he died in 1630, probably as a result of the plague that ravaged Europe that year. The dates that Fétis gives for Andrea Amati's grandson Nicolò, September 3, 1596 and August 12, 1684, are properly December 3, 1596 and April 12, 1684. Fétis makes no mention of the last violin-making member of the Amati family, Nicolò's son Girolamo II, who was born on February 26, 1649 and died on February 21, 1740.

Fétis gives Stradivari's birth year as 1644, a date based upon a hand-written notation of his age, 92, that the maker purportedly wrote on a printed violin label dated 1736. Some historians have called this inscription into question, as well as other handwritten notations found on Stradivari's labels, though the birth year of 1644 is still generally accepted despite the fact no birth or baptismal record has been found in Cremonese church archives. Curiously, though the Stradivari surname goes back many centuries in census books and other public records preserved in Cremona, there is no apparent link between those earlier members of the Stradivari family and the violin maker named Antonio. Fétis states that Antonio Stradivari was a pupil of Nicolò Amati, which is still considered an indisputable fact by many violin experts, although Stradivari's name is not listed in the census returns of the Amati household, as are the names of other apprentices and workers.

Fétis' analysis of Stradivari's work and stylistic development is somewhat superficial, though the section on acoustics is of considerable interest. Fétis dismisses an old saw: that the passage of time is responsible for the tonal excellence of instruments made by Stradivari and Giuseppe Guarneri del Gesù. As evidence, he points out that instruments made by other makers who worked as far back as the seventeenth century do not possess the tonal quality of those made by these two legendary figures, despite the passage of time. Fétis then summarizes the groundbreaking experimental work carried out by contemporary physicists Felix Savart and Ernst Chladni. Their researches into the resonant frequencies of the top and bottom plates of the violin, the resonance of the air enclosed within the violin's body, as well as the acoustical function of the F-holes, remain essentially unchallenged to this day. The advent of hologram interferometry, acoustical holography, and acoustical spectrum analysis, as well as new branches of mathematics such as modal and finite element analysis (which in recent years have been brought to bear in the study of violin acoustics) have not contributed much to the practice of violin making, and most modern makers still resort to tapping the front and back plates with their fingertips to ascertain their resonant frequencies during the carving process. In a section devoted to the development of the violin bridge, Fétis presents drawings of five bridges. He attributes the modern form of the bridge to Stradivari, but that design did not come into use until around 1815 and was probably developed in France. Fétis' Figure 3 is closer in style to Stradivari's bridges that are preserved in the Museo Stradivariano in Cremona.

The Stradivari monograph includes a list of his "pupils." With the exception of his sons Francesco and Omobono, the other members of this list should be considered "followers" rather than those who trained with or worked in Stradivari's shop, as no assistants are listed in his census returns. Fétis then lists fifteen Italian makers whom he terms "of the third class" and touches on a few non-Italian makers of note: Germans Jacob Stainer and members of the Klotz families, as well the French makers Lupot and Vuillaume. Jacob Stainer's birth year is given as 1620, whereas 1618–1619 is perhaps a better estimate. Certain facts about Stainer should be called into question, such as his alleged apprenticeship with the Amatis and his collaboration with a brother named Marcus. Fétis here states that Stainer made a dozen special instruments that he presented to the electors of the Holy Roman Empire (in his remarks about Stainer in his earlier Paganini monograph he indicates that Stainer made sixteen such instruments: twelve presented to the electors and four given to the emperor of the Holy Roman Empire); however, the whereabouts of these instruments are unknown and recent research has yielded no documentary evidence of these supposed gifts. It is important to keep in mind that this historical essay was written before the publication of comparatively well-researched biographical dictionaries of violin makers, such as Willibald Leo Freiherrn von Lütgendorff's *Die Geigen- und Lautenmacher vom Mittelalter bis zur Gegenwart* (Frankfurt, 1904). Previously, biographical information about violin makers had been deduced by dealers (such as Fétis' consultant Vuillaume), who reconstructed birth, death, and dates of activity from authentic violin labels (which were formerly in greater abundance than today).

Following his discussion of Stradivari, Fétis provides a short essay on the Guarneri family. He states that Andrea (Andrew here) was born in the early seventeenth century and was one of the first pupils of Nicolò Amati. More precisely, Andrea was born in 1623 and is listed as a *garzone*, or shop boy, in the earliest known census return of Nicolò Amati, dated 1641, through the census return of 1653. Fétis does not include a date of death for Andrea Guarneri (he indicates that he was active through 1695), though we now know he died in 1698. The dates given for Andrea's sons Giuseppe (Joseph; popularly known as "Joseph filius Andreæ") and Pietro (Peter; known as "Peter of Mantua") are incorrect: they are more properly 1666–1740 for Giuseppe and 1655–1720 for Peter. Regarding Giuseppe's son Pietro, Fétis gives no dates (he was born in 1695 and died in 1762) and simply states that he worked in Cremona between 1725 and 1740. In fact, this Pietro left Cremona around 1717 to work in Venice, first in the workshop of Matteo Sellas between the years 1717 and 1733 and then as an independent maker. He has long been known as "Peter of Venice," and it is odd that the workplace of this important maker eluded Fétis.

We then come to the most highly esteemed member of the family: Giuseppe Guarneri—often referred to as "del Gesù" because the cross and initials IHS (the Christian symbol and monogram for Jesus) are printed on his violin labels. Fétis refers to him as "Joseph Anthony," though he was christened Bartolomeo Giuseppe. Regarding del Gesù's date of birth, Fétis and others during his time were likely confused by the birth records of two of his brothers who were both christened Joseph Antonio, one who passed away in 1683 and another who died as a two-day old infant in 1702. Fétis indicates that Vuillaume's researches had uncovered an authentic document revealing del Gesù's year of birth as 1683; however, this was the birth record of one of the brothers named Joseph Antonio noted above. Church records indicate that the maker we now know as del Gesù was born in 1698. Fétis deduced that he died in 1745, probably on the basis of the date on the label of one of his most famous violins known as the "Leduc"; however, church records indicate that he passed away in 1744. The "Leduc" is now thought to have been completed and dated posthumously by del Gesù's wife Catarina, primarily on the basis of Fétis' statement that del Gesù was assisted by his wife. Fétis credits a descendent of the violin maker Carlo Bergonzi with this revelation. Carlo Bergonzi was not only a contemporary of del Gesù but lived next door to him and could have readily observed this collaboration; the descendent who most likely transmitted this information was his grandson, the violin maker Carlo Bergonzi II (1757–1836). Finally, Fétis conveys the oft repeated tale of del Gesù's purported imprisonment at the end of his life, during which time he is said to have made violins using wood smuggled into his cell by the jailor's daughter. Recent research in the civil archives of Cremona has failed to confirm the story of his imprisonment.

Included in this monograph is a chapter entitled "The Bow of Francis Tourte," in which Fétis recounts the historical development of the bow, with particular reference to the work of François-Xavier Tourte, otherwise known as Tourte *le jeune* (Tourte the younger). He introduces this topic with a brief history of the bow, illustrating it with depictions of eight examples dating from 1620 to 1790 and concluding that "no serious attempt was made to improve the bow until towards the middle of the eighteenth century." After a discussion of the work of François-Xavier Tourte's father (known as Tourte *père*), his older brother (known as Tourte *l'aîné*, or Tourte the elder), and a brief biography of François-Xavier himself, Fétis turns his attention to the latter's development of the modern bow and his technique of bow making. His consultant in the matter was once again Vuillaume, whose shop was but a short distance from Tourte's premises on the quai de l'École. Fétis' report on Tourte's working methods is thus of considerable historical interest, though certain elements of it, such as the formula derived by Vuillaume for the expansion of the bow's radius over its length ($y = -3.11 + 2.57 \log x$), were speculative—in fact, the radii of Tourte's bows rarely conform precisely to the dimensions calculated by this equation.

Three appendices are included in the monograph. The first two consist of a transcription and translation of one of the two known letters by Stradivari. The letter, which is addressed to a "most esteemed, reverend, and illustrious Sir" and dated August 2, 1708, is a bill for restoration work. In it, Stradivari begs the pardon of his client for the delay in completing the restoration because the varnish had to dry. This statement has been thought to indicate that Stradivari used an oil varnish, which required prolonged exposure to sunlight to assist in the oxidation of the drying oil. This conclusion has recently been confirmed by the chemical analyses of several chips of Stradivari's varnish, which indicate that it consists of a simple combination of linseed oil and pine resin with some pigments added to provide color. The third appendix consists of Vuillaume's immodest account of his repair of Paganini's famous Guarneri violin, the so-called "Cannon," and Paganini's purported glowing reception of a copy that Vuillaume made of it.

Reproduced in this Dover edition is Vuillaume's advertisement for violins and bows that was printed on the next to the last page of the original English edition. This advertisement is of considerable interest because Vuillaume claims to have used old wood "sought out with much labor and at great expense, amongst the weather-beaten chalets of Switzerland" to impart the "requisite qualities of age and consequent resonance." This contradicts the assertion made in Fétis' discussion of acoustics—that the passage of time does not increase the acoustic quality of violins. If in fact Vuillaume did construct his instruments out of old wood, this would confound those who employ the wood-dating technique of dendrochronology to distinguish his copies from authentic Cremonese instruments. The famous violin known as "The Messiah" (preserved in the Ashmolean Museum in Oxford) would appear to be such a copy.

Though certain details (notably birth and death dates) have been revised in recent years, this slender volume contains a wealth of information about the origin and development of the violin, Stradivari's work, and the work of the bow maker François-Xavier Tourte, who in his day was referred to as "the Stradivarius of the bow."

STEWART POLLENS

CONTENTS.

Editor's Preface xx
Author's Preface xxii
Introduction—Anthony Stradivari, known by the name of
    Stradivarius, the celebrated violin-maker; his pre-
    decessors, contemporaries, and pupils xiv
Historical researches on the origin and transformations of
    bow-instruments 1
Violin-makers of the Italian school from the earliest times 45
Anthony Stradivarius—improvements of bow-instruments 61
The Guarneri or Guarnerius [family] 101
The bow of Francis Tourte 109
Experimental determination of the form of Tourte's bows . 121

APPENDIX,

BY THE EDITOR.

No. I—Letter of Anthony Stradivari, deciphered from the
    fac-simile 127
No. II—Translation of the preceding letter 128
No. III—Some account of Paganini's celebrated Guarnerius
    violin (mentioned at p. 106). 129

EDITOR'S PREFACE.

IN presenting this interesting work to the English public, an acknowledgment is due both to the learned Author, for his kindness in allowing the translation to be made, and also to M. Vuillaume for his courteous replies to certain enquiries which it was deemed necessary to submit to him.

Respect for the labours of M. Fétis in the various departments of musical literature, and the special importance attaching to the history of bow-instruments, as illustrated in the following sheets, have created a desire on the part of the Editor to render the sense of the original in as scrupulously faithful a manner as possible. Where any uncertainty prevailed, the translation here offered will be found to include, in parentheses, the terms or phrases employed by the Author himself; and any additions which appeared desirable for the elucidation of the text have been introduced either within brackets, or as foot notes.

It is therefore hoped that this edition will be acceptable both to violinists and performers on kindred instruments, and also to musicians generally.

J. B.

Cheltenham,
 July 20, 1864.

AUTHOR'S PREFACE.

PASSIONATELY fond of his art, like every man of sterling worth, M. Vuillaume has conceived a degree of admiration, amounting almost to devotion, for Anthony Stradivarius, the celebrated violin-maker of Cremona, whose long career was wholly dedicated to seeking and realising perfection in the construction of bow-instruments.

After having spent a part of his life in studying the principles which guided this great artist in his labours, M. Vuillaume wished to raise a monument to his memory, and took several journeys into Italy, for the sole object of collecting the requisite materials. On becoming possessed of these, he entrusted them to me, and requested my co-operation for his truly reverential work.

Although foreign to the habitual nature of my studies, this occupation presented much of interest to me, like everything that concerns the art to which I have devoted my life. Enlightened by the experience of M. Vuillaume, I have been enabled to render myself sufficiently familiar with the technical details of the manufacture of bow-instruments, to speak of them, I hope, with clearness. This, then, with the exception of what relates to the origin of these instruments, is all that belongs to me in the present little publication.

FÉTIS.

Brussels, May 8, 1856.

INTRODUCTION.

ANTHONY STRADIVARI,

KNOWN BY THE NAME OF

STRADIVARIUS,

THE CELEBRATED VIOLIN-MAKER;

HIS PREDECESSORS, CONTEMPORARIES, AND PUPILS.

ITALY, the fertile land of great and beautiful things; Italy, which preceded all the nations of Europe in civilisation; Italy, in short, which has been endowed with every species of glory in poetry, philosophy, science and the arts; Italy, I say, has given birth to the artists who have carried the manufacture of musical instruments of the bow kind to the highest degree of perfection. From the middle of the fifteenth century, this art was already cultivated there with success. From whence did it come?

By what progressive causes was it developed, until it had attained its utmost limits under the hands of Anthony Stradivarius and those of Joseph Guarnerius, surnamed *del Jesù?* Why has it degenerated among their successors? Such are the problems which I propose to examine carefully in this work, and of which I hope to present the solution, as well from an historical as from a theoretical point of view.

HISTORICAL RESEARCHES

ON THE ORIGIN AND TRANSFORMATIONS OF

BOW-INSTRUMENTS.

WHAT is the origin of bow-instruments? This archæological problem has engaged the attention of many learned men, without their having arrived at a satisfactory solution. Certain obscure expressions, interpreted in an unnatural manner, have induced the belief that the Greeks and Romans possessed, among their instruments of music, something which resembled the viol. Some have fancied they recognized it in the *magadis*—the name of which is derived from *magas* (a bridge)—because nothing like a bridge appears in the lyres and cytharas.

The magadis was mounted with twenty strings, or with twenty-one according to Athenæus, or twenty-two according to Pausanias. John Baptist Doni thought it might have borne some analogy with the *viola di Bordone*, otherwise called *lirone*, which was used in Italy in the sixteenth century, and the eleven or twelve strings of which served to produce arpeggios with the bow, or harmony in many parts. These conjectures, however, have no historical value, being unsupported by any passage in the ancient writers; neither does any monument among the Greeks present us with an instrument having a neck and a bridge.

Some have been disposed to trace the bow in the *plectrum;* but πλῆκτρον comes from πλήσσειν, *to strike.* The dictionaries, it is true, define it as *the bow of a musical instrument;* but this arises from a confusion in regard to the real meaning of the word. Statues, bas-reliefs, and the pictures on Greek vases, afford us numerous representations of the plectrum; but in all we see a piece of wood, bone, or ivory, ending with little hooks to pull the strings, or to strike them with the back. Had the Greeks wished to describe a veritable bow, the hairs of which serve, by friction, to put the strings into vibration, they would have called it τοξάριον (*little bow*). But nothing like a bow appears in any Greek or Roman sculpture or painting which has come down to us.

The country which affords us the most ancient memorials of a perfect language, of an advanced civilization, of a philosophy where all directions of human thought find their expression, of a poesy immensely rich in every style, and of a musical art corresponding with the lively sensibility of the people—India, appears to have given birth to bow-instruments, and to have made them known to other parts of Asia, and afterwards to Europe. There, no conjecture is needed, for the instruments themselves exist, and still preserve the characteristics of their native originality. If we would trace a bow-instrument to its source, we must assume the most simple form in which it could appear, and such as required no assistance from an art brought to perfection. Such a form we shall find in the *ravanastron*, made of a cylinder of sycamore wood, hollowed out from one end to the other. This cylinder is 11 centimètres* [4.331 inches Eng.] long, and has a diameter of 5 centimètres [1.969 in.]. Over one end is stretched a piece of *boa* skin, with large scales, which forms the belly or sound-board. The cylinder is crossed from side to side—at one-third of its length, next the sound-board—by a rod or shank of deal, which serves as a neck, of the length of 55 centimètres [21.654 in.], rounded on its under part, but flat on the top, and slightly inclined backwards. The head of this neck is pierced with two holes for the pegs, 12 millimètres [.472 in.] in diameter; not in the side, but in the plane of the sound-board. Two large pegs, 10 centimètres [3.937 in.] in length—shaped hexagonally at the top, and rounded at the ends which go into the holes—serve to tighten two strings made of the intestines of the Gazelle, which are fixed to a strap of serpent skin attached to the lower extremity of the rod or shank. A little bridge, 18 millimètres [.709 in.] long, cut sloping on the top, but flat on the part which rests on the sound-board, and worked out rectangularly in this part, so as to form two separate feet: this supports the strings. As to the bow, it is formed of a small bamboo, of which the upper portion is slightly curved, and the lower straight. A hole is made in the

---

* Approximate values in English measures are given within brackets, retaining only two or three decimal places.—TR.

head of the bow, at the first knot, for fastening a hank of hair, which is strained and fixed at the other end, by binding a very flexible rush string twenty times round it.

Such is the primitive bow-instrument, now abandoned to people of the lowest class, and to the poor Buddhist monks, who go from door to door asking alms. Its sound is sweet, though muffled. According to Indian tradition, it was invented by Ravana, King of Ceylon, five thousand years before the Christian era.

Other instruments, made in imitation of the *ravanastron*, are known among the poorer classes of Hindostan. The first, which we may consider as the base of that, is also made of a cylinder of sycamore, 16 centimètres [6.299 in.] long, and 11 centimètres [4.331 in.] in diameter, and hollowed throughout its length; so that the thickness of this sonorous body does not exceed 3 millimètres [.118 in.]. This body is crossed from side to side by a rod or shank of the total length of 86 centimètres [33.858 in.], which forms the neck, as in the *ravanastron*. A hole is bored vertically, at the lower extremity of this shank, into which is inserted a little pin of iron-wood, 9 centimètres [3.543 in.] long, terminated by a knob or button, which carries a strap of jackall leather, to which the strings are attached. The sound-board is formed of a thin plate of mounah-wood, which, in its longitudinal fibres, bears a resemblance to deal. This instrument, which is called the *rouana*, is mounted with two strings, like the *ravanastron*, to which it is in all other respects similar.

To an epoch doubtless posterior to the invention of

the two instruments before mentioned belongs the *omerti*, another bow-instrument, mounted with two strings, and which evinces some progress in the art of manufacture. The body is made of a cocoa-nut shell, one-third being first cut away, and after reducing its thickness to 2 millimètres [.079 in.], it is then polished inside and out. Four elliptical openings, and another of a lozenge form, are cut in the front part of the body, to serve as soundholes. I possess two of these instruments; in one of them the sound-board is formed of a piece of Gazelle skin, well prepared and very smooth; in the other it consists of a veneer of satin-wood, extremely fine in the grain, and 1 millimètre [.03937 in.] thick. In both instruments, the size of this sound-board at its greatest diameter is 0^m,05,15 [2.027 in.]. As in the *ravanastron* and the *rouana*, the neck is formed of a shank of deal (red wood of India), which passes through the body of the instrument. The lower part is rounded, and a hole is bored longitudinally at the bottom, to receive a pin, ending in a knob or button, as in the *rouana*. This button is a little cube, having a hole in it where the strings are fastened. The upper part of the neck is flat, and terminates in a head turned back and finished off at right angles with the neck. The pegs are not placed upon this head, but both are inserted on the left of the neck, and a longitudinal opening is made through the head, 6 centimètres [2.362 in.] in length, and 12 millimètres [.472 in.] wide, for passing the strings into the holes of the pegs: this is a rude commencement of the *scroll*. Lastly, at the lower end of the opening is a little ivory nut, 1 millimètre [.03937 in.] in height, on which the strings rest. The bridge, over which they pass at the other end, is exactly like that of the *ravanastron*. The bow, which is longer than that of the latter instrument, is also made of a light bamboo, which forms the curved part. At its upper end is a slit in which the hank of hair is fixed; but, instead of being fastened by a rush string at the other end, it passes through a hole in the bamboo, and is there stayed by a knot.

If we compare the *omerti* with the Arabian instrument called *kemángeh à gouz* (from *kemán*, a bow, and *káh*, pronounced *guiáh*, place; that is to say, *place of the bow*, or *bow-instrument*), we shall immediately perceive that the Indian instrument has furnished the model for that of Arabia. The expression *à gouz* signifies *ancient;* from whence it follows that *kemángeh à gouz* answers to *ancient bow-instrument*, or *primitive bow-instrument*. The lexicons translate كمانجة, *kemángeh*, by *viol*. Villoteau remarks that this word is Persian*. Now, ancient Persia was contiguous to India on the east, and the relations of these two great countries are apparent throughout history. I affirm that it is impossible to forget the *omerti* in the *kemángeh à gouz;* a mere glance at the latter being sufficient to reveal their identity. The body of both instruments is formed of a cocoa-nut shell, with one-third part cut off; openings are made in the body of the *kemángeh*, as in that of the *omerti*, for putting the exterior air into communication with that which is contained in the instrument; the only differ-

---

* *Description historique, technique, et littéraire des instruments de musique des Orientaux*, in the great *Description de l'Egypte*, tome xiii, p. 290, of the 8vo edition.

ence being that these openings are small, very numerous, and ranged symmetrically in the Arabian instrument. In this, as in the other, the belly or sound-board consists of fine skin glued to the edges of the cocoa-nut shell. The neck consists of a cylindrical shank of courbary wood, its lower part terminating in a large ivory ferrule. The length of this shank, from the body of the instrument to the commencement of the head, is 66 centimètres [25.984 in.]. The head, which is hollowed out for the two pegs, like that of the *omerti*, is made of a single piece of ivory, 20 centimètres long [7.874 in.]. The pegs are placed one on each side of the head, instead of being both on the left as in the Indian instrument. The shank is bored longitudinally, to receive an iron rod, which crosses the body of the instrument, and, instead of ending in a button, like the *omerti*, is extended outwards, to the length of 25 centimètres [9.842 in.], to form a foot. To this foot there is a hook, to which is fastened the ring which serves for a tail-piece. In the description of this instrument, Villoteau speaks of the finger-board*; but there is nothing like it on the *kemângeh à gouz* which is in my collection: the cylindrical neck itself serves for the finger-board†, as in the *omerti*. The strings are the most curious part of this instrument, each of them being formed of a hank of black hair highly stretched. The bow is composed of a rod of

---

* *Description historique, technique, et littéraire des instruments de musique des Orientaux*, before mentioned.

† Such also is the case in the representations of this instrument given in vol. ii of Lane's *Manners and Customs of the Modern Egyptians*. Knight's small edit.—TR.

sycamore fig-tree *(figuier-sycomore)*, worked round and then curved, to which is attached and stretched a hank of the same hair [as that used for the strings].

The instruments already described fall not, properly speaking, within the domain of art; they belong to music of a primitive and popular kind, the instinctive expression of a feeling which has everywhere preceded genuine art. In the same category must be ranged, as mere varieties, certain other instruments made on the same principle, the diversity in the forms of which appears to have originated only in fancy. Such is the *rebáb* of the Arabs, which does not enter into any combination of instruments used at concerts in eastern countries, and which serves no other purpose than to guide the voice of the poets and story-tellers in their chanted recitations. The body of the *rebáb* consists of four sides, on which are stretched two pieces of parchment, which thus form the belly and the back. This combination of parts presents the appearance of a trapezoid, of which the summit is parallel to the base, and the two sides are nearly equal. The neck is cylindrical, and formed of a single piece, including the head. The foot consists of an iron rod fixed into the neck, which passes through the instrument. The *rebáb* is placed on this foot, like the *kemángeh à gouz*. There are two kinds of *rebáb*, both of which have the same form: the first is called the *poet's rebáb*, and has only one string; the other, which has two, is named the *singer's rebáb*. To say the truth, the *rebáb* is nothing but a modification of the Indian *rouana*—a modification which consists only in the form of the body of the instrument. The *rebáb* does not appertain to music, properly speaking; it is confined to its primary use of sustaining the voice, by rubbing the string with the bow*.

If we now turn to Europe, and there examine the oldest monuments, together with the earliest particulars collected on the subject of bow-instruments, we shall find in them the same traces of Indian origin. *There is nothing in the West which has not come from the East.* In many places of my writings I have stated this truth, and now again repeat it. Formerly, I thought it admitted of a single exception as regards the bow, whose origin I had observed in the *goudok* of the Russian peasantry†; but, at that time, I had only a very imperfect knowledge of India, in a musical point of view. Favorable circumstances, however, which, during the lapse of twenty years, have enabled me to fully investigate the ancient musical doctrines of this country, and which have brought into my possession a portion of its native instruments,—these circumstances, I say, have enlightened me; so that I can now reiterate, without any reservation, *there is nothing in the West which has not come from the East.* The *goudok*—with its three strings, its scroll, its finger-board placed on the neck, its regularly constructed sonorous chest, its sound-holes in the belly, its bridge duly proportioned to the length of the strings, its tail-piece similar to that of our violins—is a

---

* Representations of this instrument may be seen in Lane's work before referred to.—Tr.

† See my *Résumé philosophique de l'histoire de la musique*, at the commencement of the first volume of the *Biographie universelle des Musiciens*, p. cxxix, 1st edition.

viol already brought to perfection, and does not resemble a primitive essay. The *goudok* also derives its origin from the East.

No traces of the existence of bow-instruments appear on the continent of Europe before the end of the eighth or the beginning of the ninth century; but a poet— Venantius Fortunatus, Bishop of Poictiers, who died about 609, and who is thought to have composed his elegiac poems about 570—tells us that the *crŵth* or *crouth* of the Gaelic [? Celtic] or Welsh bards was then known, and that it probably existed in England a long while before. The poet renders this barbarous name by *chrotta*, in the following verses :

> Romanusque lyra plaudat tibi, Barbarus harpa,
> Græcus achilliaca, chrotta Britanna canat.*

---

* " Let the Roman applaud thee with the lyre, the Barbarian with the harp, the Greek with the *phorminx of Achilles* (?) [a]; let the British crouth sing [to thee]." These verses, addressed to Loup, Duke of Champagne, the friend of Fortunatus (*Carm.* 8, lib. vii), are specimens of the habitual poetic exaggeration of these barbarous times. I know not why Du Cange has substituted the word *placet* for *canat* in quoting these verses (*Gloss. ad script. mediæ et infim. ætatis*, voc. *Chrotta*). He corrects an error in quantity [? TR.] in the first verse, giving it thus;

> Romanus lyra plaudat tibi, Barbarus harpa.

Nothing is more amusing than the note of the Jesuit Brower, editor of the works of Venantius Fortunatus, on the word *chrotta (Notæ diversæ*, p. 186), which, says he, has an evident affinity with *crotale*. Yet he thinks that the instrument referred to must have borne some resemblance to the shell of the tortoise, the name of which, in ancient German, was *crotte* or *krote*, from whence originated the name of a shield in the form of a tortoise, *schildkrote!*—AUTHOR.

---

[a] M. Fétis having rendered the word *Achilliaca* by *la cithare*, and his translation being in other respects different from mine, I subjoin his own version, in order that he may not be held responsible for what does not belong to him:

" Le Romain t'applaudit sur la lyre, le Grec te chante avec la cithare, le Barbare avec la harpe et le crouth breton."—TR.

The Saxons took possession of a part of England in the year 449, that is to say, upwards of a century before the period in which Venantius Fortunatus wrote his poems. We know that they governed the part of Great Britain which was subdued by them; for their predecessors, the Romans, were only encamped there. It might be supposed that the use of a bow-instrument was introduced by them among the Britons; but we must not forget that Wales was never brought under the Saxon rule, and that the *crouth*, the use of which appears to have been preserved to the descendants of the Celts, seems to have been long unknown to the other people of England. The name of the instrument is evidently Celtic, and the original orthography of the word (crŵth) cannot belong to any other language than the Gaelic.* Now, the Welsh *w*, with an accent, has precisely the sound of the vowel ऋ (*ŭ*) of the Sanscrit language. Edward Jones, bard to the Prince of Wales, remarks that *crouth*, or *crowd*, is an English alteration of the primitive word, from whence is derived *crowther*, or *crowder*, to play on the *crouth*.† The Welsh name of the instrument (crŵth) comes from the Celtic primitive

---

* The frequent use of the term *Gaelic*, in this part of the work, seems considerably to impair the author's meaning; it being presumed he has no intention of alluding to the Highlanders of Scotland, or their language.

A friend, deeply versed in the language and antiquities of Wales, and who is also a native of the Principality, suggests that the little inconsistencies here observable have doubtless been induced through the inaccuracies in foreign works, particularly French, in reference to details of Welsh history. It is therefore hoped that these remarks, together with a few interpolations within brackets, will shield the learned author from being misunderstood.—TR.

† See *A Dissertation on the Musical Instruments of the Welsh*, p. 114, Note 2.

cruisigh (music), which is itself derived from the Sanscrit *krus'* (to cry out, to produce loud sounds), the root of which is *kur* (to yield a sound).*

The *Gaelic Kymri*, who originally peopled *Kymbery* [? *Kymru*] or *Cambria*, now Wales, were a Celtic colony which issued from Gaul; for *Gaels*, *Galli*, *Gauls* and *Welsh* are identical terms, and refer to one and the same people. The Gaelic [? Celtic] language which they spoke, and which they still speak in the mountain districts, differs but little from the Celtic dialect in use among the Low Britons of France. Now, in the present state of ethnographical knowledge, the Indo-Germanic origin of the Celts is no longer contested. At epochs anterior to all historical records, and by slow migrations, the European races have advanced from India through Bactriana, Persia, Arabia, and Armenia; then, after having crossed the Hellespont (the present Dardanelles), they have invaded the vast countries now known by the names of Roumelia, Transylvania, Wallachia, Servia, Sclavonia, Croatia, Hungary, Styria, and Bohemia. Subsequently, when pressed by other masses of people arrived by the same route, they have abandoned these

---

* This etymology seems incontrovertible. (See Pictet, *de l'Affinité des langues celtiques avec le sanscrit*, pp. 21 and 64.) As to that proposed by Edward Jones (*loc. cit.*) in deriving *crwth* from *croth*, which, in the Gaelic [? Celtic] language, signifies the calf of the leg, the womb, and also vessel for holding water, and which resembles the Syriac word *cruth*, and the Greek χροσσὸς, the signification of which is the same, I confess I do not understand the analogy.—AUTHOR.

[Ed. Jones's words are these: " *Croth*, or *Crŵth*, by the Britons, signifies the calf of the leg, the womb, or belly; as also by the Syrians כרח (*Crath*), and by the Grecians Κρωσσὸς, signifies the womb, or a water-vessel.—*Baxter's Glossarium Antiquitatum Britannicarum*, p. 92. And *Richards's Welsh Dictionary*."]—TR.

stations in order to disperse themselves in various directions, crossing the great rivers, such as the Danube, the Elbe, the Rhine, the Saône, and the Meuse; in short, peopleing, by one of their branches, the whole of Gaul, under the name of *Celts*, and sub-dividing themselves into an infinity of tribes continually at war with one another. This, however, is not the place to point out the traces more or less authentic—more or less certain of these relationships : some learned men of the greatest eminence have acquitted themselves of this task, in modern times, in a manner altogether special. Linguistic science, too, has thrown a light on these questions, and triumphed over the most obstinate incredulity. Music, the universal expression of the affections of the soul, can also furnish its auxiliary proofs, as I shall show elsewhere. But, in connection with the present subject, we have only to trace the analogies between the bow-instruments of the West and the primitive type which we have seen in India, and then to verify the transformations and the progress of them.

A question here presents itself: is the *crouth* (the two forms of which we shall presently show) an instrument invented by the Britons, as certain English and Welsh antiquaries pretend, especially the bard Edward Jones; or is it simply an improvement of a previous rude model? At the first view, this problem appears to be resolved by the expression of Venantius Fortunatus, *chrotta Britanna* (the *British crouth*) ; but, independently of Britons and Gaels existing in France, as well as in England, there is substantial ground for rejecting the immediate invention of such an instrument as the *crouth*, even in its simplest form; because the idea of a sonorous chest, consisting of a belly, back and sides, with a neck, several strings raised by a bridge and attached by iron pegs to the back of the head—the idea, I say, of such an instrument, cannot be primitive. One can understand the invention of the Indian *ravanastron;* because such a rude type might be the work of the first person who should accidentally discover that a skein of thread twisted, a piece of wood, and a metallic rod, produce sounds when they are put into vibration by rubbing them with horse-hair; but one cannot conceive that an instrument whose construction requires the skill of a violin-maker was contrived, as a first essay, in times of barbarism. There is, then, every reason to believe that the Indo-Celtic race, in its migrations, transported the shapeless model of the apparatus with fretted strings (*l'appareil à cordes frottées*) which, in its highest state of perfection, now charms us in the hands of the *virtuosi*. The principle of the production of sounds by the action of the bow might doubtless have been discovered in different places; but a regularly constructed instrument could not have been produced at once by a people little advanced in civilization, who lived under a rigorous climate; whilst its origin in India is only marked by feeble essays. The very remarkable affinities of the Sanscrit and the Celtic dialects are certain indications of the primitive relationship of these nations, so widely separated from each other.

Be that as it may, there were two kinds of *crouth*, which belong to different periods. The oldest of them is the *crouth trithant*, that is, the crouth with three strings; which is probably the one referred to by Venantius Fortunatus. Perhaps even this primitive *crouth* had [at first] but two strings; as was the case, long afterwards, with other instruments which will be mentioned farther on. A manuscript of the eleventh century, formerly belonging to the Abbey of Saint Martial de Limoges, but now in the Imperial Library, Paris (No. 1118 of the Latin MSS.), contains some representations of instruments, very rudely designed, among which there occurs the figure of a crowned personage, who holds in his left hand a *crouth* with three strings, which he plays with the bow in his right, as here shown:

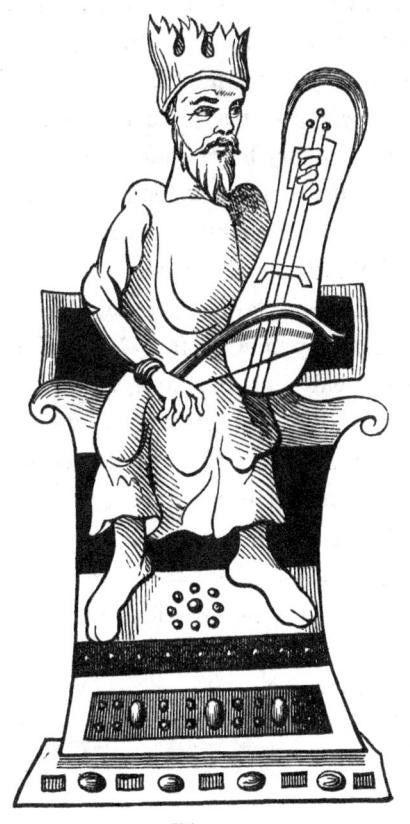

Fig. 1.

The instrument is known by the opening through which the hand passes for placing the fingers on the strings. Another representation of the *crouth trithant* is seen among the exterior ornaments of Melross Abbey, in Scotland, which was built at the commencement of the fourteenth century, in the reign of Edward the Second; consequently it was still in use at that period.

On the 3rd of May, 1770, Daines Barrington, then judge of the counties of Caernarvon and Anglesey, in Wales, read, at a meeting of the Society of Antiquaries in London, of which he was a member, some remarks on two instruments used in that country—the *crouth* and the *pib-corn;* they were published in the third volume of the *Archæologia**, with a plate representing the two instruments, on a very large scale, to render the details intelligible. Although a little too summary, the remarks of Daines Barrington are interesting, because he had not only seen the instruments of which he speaks, but had also heard the *crouth* played by John Morgan, who was born in the Isle of Anglesey, in 1711, and was then 59 years of age, and who appeared to be the last bard capable of playing this instrument, which had become excessively rare. The figure of the *crouth* given by Daines Barrington was drawn from the instrument itself. Bottée de Toulmont has had a bad copy made of it, for his *Dissertation on the Musical Instruments used in the Middle Ages*†, which gives false ideas of the construction

---

* *Archæologia, or Miscellaneous tracts relating to Antiquity; published by the Society of Antiquaries, of London.* Vol. iii, p. 32. 1775.

† *Dissertation sur les instruments de musique employés au moyen âge,* in vol. xvii of the *Mémoires de la Société royale des Antiquaires de France.*

of the *crouth*. M. Coussemaker has done more: in reproducing the bad figure of Bottée de Toulmont, instead of reverting to the *Archæologia*, he writes beneath this new copy: *crout à six cordes.—Mss. du XI*ᵉ. *siècle.** Now, it is neither a matter which concerns a manuscript —since the instrument was drawn from nature—nor the eleventh century; for it relates to an instrument comparatively modern and brought to perfection, which existed towards the end of the eighteenth century. This blunder is tantamount to presenting the harp with three rows of strings, as now used by the bards of Caernarvon and Merioneth, for that of the sixth century of which Venantius Fortunatus speaks.

To determine the epoch when the *crouth* with six strings succeeded the *crouth trithant*, would be impossible; for no positive information on this subject has been discovered up to the present time†. The first had not ceased to exist when the other became adopted, since the bard, Edward Jones, informs us that it was less esteemed, because it could not produce such full

---

* *Essai sur les instruments de musique du moyen âge*, in the *Annales archéologiques*, published by Didron Sen., vol. iii, p. 150.

† " We have," says Mr. Bingley, " no authentic information respecting the crŵth of more ancient date than the fifteenth century."— *North Wales, including its scenery, antiquities, customs, &c.* vol. ii, p. 332.

The information referred to by this learned writer is doubtless the description of the instrument with six strings by the Welsh bard, Graffyd Davydd ab Howel, who really lived in the fifteenth century, and the original of which is subjoined, together with an English version, from the work of Edward Jones (*loc. cit.* p. 115).

Crŵth.

Prennol têg bŵa a gwregis,   A fair coffer with a bow, a girdle,
Pont a brân, punt yw ei brîs;   a finger-board, and a bridge; its
    value is a pound;

harmony.* The admirable construction of the *crouth* with six strings, which the same author and Daines Barrington have described, shows that the art of manufacturing stringed instruments had greatly advanced among the Welsh at the period when crouths were made. These instruments have the form of an elongated trapezoid, the length of which, from top to bottom, is 57 centimètres [22.441 in.]; the greatest width, near the tailpiece, is 27 centimètres [10.63 in.], and the least, at the top of the trapezium, is 23 centimètres [9.055 in.]. The thickness of the sonorous chest, composed of a back and a belly of sycamore, united by sides, is 5 centimètres [1.968 in.], and the length of the finger-board

A thalaith ar waith olwyn,	it has a frontlet formed like a wheel,
A'r bwa ar draws byr ei drwyn,	with the short-nosed bow across;
Ac o'i ganol mae dolen,	and from its centre it winds in a ring,
A gwàr hwn megis gŵr hên;	and the bulging of its back is somewhat like an old man;
Ac ar ei vrest gywair vrîg,	and on its breast harmony reigns,
O'r Masarn vo geir Miwsig.	from the sycamore music will be obtained.
Chwe yspigod o's codwn,	Six pegs, if we screw them,
A dynna holl dannau hwn;	will tighten all its chords;
Chwe' thant a gaed o vantais,	six strings advantageously are found,
Ac yn y llaw yn gan llais;	which in the hand produce a hundred sounds;
Tant i bôb bys ysbys oedd,	a string for every finger is distinctly seen,
A dau-dant i'r vawd ydoedd.	and also two strings for the thumb.

From this description, we learn that the back of the *crouth* bulged; a detail which is not shown in the drawings of Daines Barrington and Jones.

* "The performers, or Minstrels of this instrument were not held in the same estimation and respect as the Bards of the *Harp* and *Crŵth*; because the three-stringed Crŵth did not admit of equal skill and harmony," &c.—See *A Dissertation on the Musical Instruments of the Welsh*, p. 116.

28 centimètres [11.023 in.]*. Of the six strings with which the instrument is mounted, two are situated off the finger-board, and are played *pizzicato* by the thumb of the left hand. The lower ends of these strings are attached to the tail-piece, which is fastened in the same way as in the ancient viols or quintons. In some instruments—for instance, in that depicted by Daines Barrington—this tail-piece presents a right line parallel to the base of the *crouth*, at the end where the strings are attached (see fig. 2, p. 22); but in others, according to the drawing given by Jones†, the tail-piece takes the oblique direction which is observed in that of the *viola bastarda (bastard viol)* with six strings, of which we shall speak farther on. The upper ends of the strings pass through holes bored in the solid top part of the instrument, rest on nuts, and are fastened at the back of the head by pegs, which are turned, says Mr. W. Bingley‡, with a key or lever, after the manner of the guitar.

Two circular sound-holes are cut in the belly, 3 centimètres [1.181 in.] in diameter. The most singular

---

* These measurements, obtained by considering the centimètre as equal to .39370 of an inch, differ from those given by Edw. Jones, which are as follow:—" The length of the Crwth is 20¼ inches, its breadth at bottom 9½; towards the top it tapers to 8 inches. Its thickness is $1\frac{8}{10}$, and the finger-board measures 10 inches in length." (*Loc. cit.* p. 115.) The dimensions of an old Crwth, in the possession of Mr. C. W. G. Wynne, as given in a recent publication, are —Length, 22 inches; width, 9¼ inches; greatest depth, 2 inches; length of finger-board, 10¼ inches.—Tr.

† *Loc. cit.* p. 89.

‡ *North Wales, including ts scenery, antiquity, customs, &c.* vol. ii, p. 331.

part of the instrument is the bridge: we cannot judge of its form from the drawing which accompanies the remarks of Daines Barrington, because the designer has not shown it in perspective; but the drawing given by Jones is satisfactory in this respect. According to the first of these authors, the bridge of the *crouth* is perfectly flat* ; W. Bingley says the same†. Edward Jones is not so definite, for he merely says that the bridge of the *crouth* is less convex at the top than that of the violin‡; however, in the figure which he gives, the top of the bridge presents a right line. The result of this, and also of the body of the instrument not having any curves in the sides for the passage of the bow, is, that the bow must touch several strings at once, and consequently produce whatever harmony is fingered. I have previously made this remark, in 1835, in my *Philosophical Summary of the History of Music.*§ Since then, M. Coussemaker has reproduced it.‖ There is another peculiarity in the bridge of the *crouth*, which imparts to it considerable interest for an intelligent observer: this consists in the inequality in the length of its feet, and in its position. Placed obliquely, in inclining towards the

---

* " The bridge of the crŵth also is perfectly flat."—(*Loc. cit.* p. 32.)

† " These (strings) are all supported by a bridge flat at the top, and not, as in the violin, convex."—(*Loc. cit.*)

‡ " The bridge of this instrument differs from that of a violin, in being less convex at the top."—*A Dissertation on the Musical Instruments of the Welsh*, p. 115.

§ *Résumé philosophique de l'histoire de la musique*, prefixed to the first edition of my *Biographie universelle des Musiciens*, vol. i, p. cxxxvii.

‖ *Essai sur les instruments de musique du moyen âge*, in the *Annales archéologiques* of Didron, vol. iii, p. 152.

right, the left foot has a length of about 7 centimètres [2.756 in.]. This foot passes through the left sound-hole into the body of the instrument, and rests on [the inside of] the back; and the right foot, whose length is about 2 centimètres [.787 in.], rests on the belly, near the right sound-hole. In consequence of this disposition, the left foot performs the functions of the sound-post in a violin, and at once puts into vibration the belly, the back, and the mass of air contained within the instrument. This placing of the bridge, which is very badly shown in the figure given by Daines Barrington, has entirely disappeared in the wretched copy of Bottée de Toulmont, and in the reproduction of it made by M. Coussemaker. In both, the oblique direction of the bridge has disappeared, as well as the inequality in the length of the feet, and the introduction of the left foot into the sound-hole: nor can we even discover in them any indication of the back of the instrument; so that it appears as if the belly were simply fitted to the sides, and that the *crouth* has no back at all. The drawing given by Edward Jones (p. 89) is very accurate; it makes the position of the left foot of the bridge perfectly intelligible, and the description which he gives of it dispels all doubt. (See *Fig.* 2, next page.*)

" The bridge is not placed at right angles with the sides of the Crwth, but in an oblique direction; and, which is farther to be remarked, one of the feet of the

---

* The figure of the crouth on the next page differs from the drawing in Jones's book, both in the shape of the bridge and in that of the tail-piece, at the end where the strings are fastened. It is a reduced copy of that given in the *Archæologia*, vol. iii.—Tr.

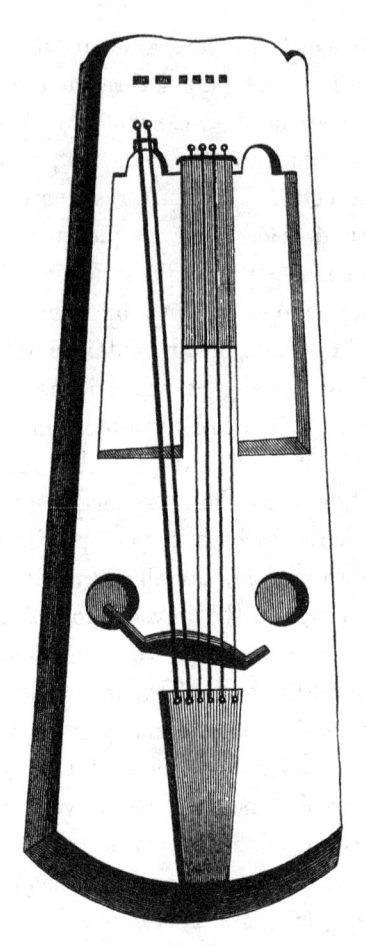

Fig. 2.

bridge serves also for a sound-post; it goes through one of the sound-holes, which are circular, and rests on the inside of the back; the other foot, which is proportionably shorter, rests on the belly before the other sound-hole." *

The six strings of the *crouth* are tuned in a peculiar manner, as follows:

---

* See *Dissertation on the Musical Instruments of the Welsh*, p. 115.

[Musical notation showing tuning: 6th, 5th, 4th, 3rd, 2nd, 1st strings]

This tuning was not chosen through mere caprice; its object was to give open notes in fifths and octaves on all the strings, whether in sounding the fifth and sixth strings *pizzicato*, or with the bow. These intervals are produced as shown in the following table:

[Musical notation table showing: Pitch-note. 1st string. | 1st & 5th strings. | 5th & 6th strings. | 1st & 2nd strings. | 3rd & 5th strings. | 3rd & 4th strings.]

It is remarkable that the sixth open string (G) sounded *pizzicato* is called *vyrdon* in the Celtic language, and that the lowest strings of bow-instruments on the continent of Europe, from the middle ages to the latter half of the eighteenth century, have been designated by the name of *bourdon*, which is evidently the same word passed into the Romance languages.

The tuning above described is that given by Daines Barrington, from the bard John Morgan, whom he heard before 1770. Edward Jones, whose interesting work was published in 1784, also gives the same tuning, which, however, may be varied to suit the key and the character of the popular melody which it is desired to perform. Thus, W. Bingley heard an old bard at Caernarvon, in 1801, who played some ancient airs on a *crouth* tuned in this manner:

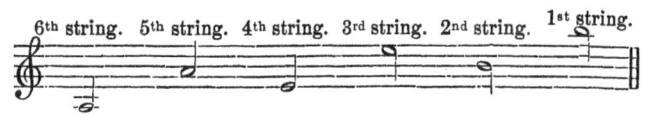

[Musical notation showing alternative tuning: 6th string, 5th string, 4th string, 3rd string, 2nd string, 1st string]

From the drawing given by Daines Barrington, we see that the sizes of the strings of the *crouth* were proportioned, as in our instruments, according to their pitch and their degree of tension. Thus, the two long strings placed on the left of the neck, and intended to be played *pizzicato*, were the largest; the strings of the low notes C and D were of a medium size, and those of the high notes of the same names were small. These distinctions have also disappeared in the copies published by Bottée de Toulmont and Coussemaker.

After what has been said concerning the *crŵth*, *crowth*, or *crouth*, it remains to examine this question:—Has this instrument exercised any influence on the origin and the transformations of bow-instruments in use on the continent of Europe, particularly on the violin? In a word, was it known there at all? What was the state of it there in the middle ages?

The words of Venantius Fortunatus which we have quoted prove that the *crouth* had appeared on the continent from the sixth century. Moreover, the figure from the manuscript of Saint Martial de Limoges shows that the primitive *crouth* with three strings was in use, in the south of France, in the eleventh century. Was this usage continued, and is the instrument traceable there in later times? On this point, Bottée de Toulmont makes conjectures, which he has fully detailed*, in order to demonstrate that an instrument called *rotta*, *rota*, *rote*, and *rothe*, by some writers in the middle ages,

---

* *Dissertation sur les instruments de musique employés au moyen âge*, p. 32 et seq.

and by the troubadours, must be synonymous with the *crouth*, whose name was altered, and not, as some have supposed, with the *hurdy-gurdy* (*vielle*), the sounds of which are produced by the friction of a wheel; because the name of the latter was *symphonie, cifonie,* or *chifonie.* Bottée de Toulmont argues from a passage in the commentary of Notker (a Monk of St. Gall, in the tenth century) on the Creed of Athanasius, a passage quoted both by Du Cange* and by Schilter†, and which poor Bottée does not understand, although the sense is perfectly clear. It refers to the ancient instrument called *psalterion,* which was mounted with ten strings and had the form of the Greek letter *delta* (Δ), and which, modified by musicians in its form and in the number of its strings, received the barbarous name of *rotta*‡. It is evident there is no reference to a bow-instrument in this passage, but to an instrument whose strings are struck or pulled, as was the case with the ancient *psalterion* or *psalterium.* There is a decisive passage, in this respect, in the 89th letter of St. Boniface, the Apostle of Germany and Archbishop of Mayence, who lived in the

---

* *Gloss. ad script. med. et infim. œtatis,* ex edit. Henschelli, vol. v, p. 786 et seq. voc. Rocta.

† *Thesaurus Antiq. Teuton,* III. *Gloss. Teuton,* voc. *Rotta.*

‡ " Sciendum est quod antiquum psalterium, instrumentum decachordum, utique erat, in hac videlicet deltæ litteræ figura multipliciter mystica. Sed postquam illud symphoniaci quidam et ludicratores, ut quidam ait, ad suum opus traxerant, formam utique ejus et figuram commoditati suæ habilem fecerant, et plures chordas annectentes et nomine barbarico *rottam* appellantes, mysticam illam Trinitatis formam transmutando."

eighth century, and perished in accomplishing his apostolic mission, June 5th, 755. " I rejoice," said he, " to have a citharist who can play on the cithara, which we call *rotta**." The *rotta, rota, rote,* or *rothe,* then, was a cithara; not the ancient cithara, which was a lyre played while resting it on the upper part of the breast (κιθαρα), but the Teutonic cithara, formed on modifications introduced into the shape of the psalterion and the number of its strings. These modifications consisted in rounding the angles of the *delta;* from which very circumstance arose its name, *rota (instrumentum rotundum*—a round instrument). We have no need to make conjectures either on the instrument itself, or on the manner of playing it; for a manuscript of the commencement of the seventh century†, which formerly existed in the library of the Abbey of St. Blaise, contained a figure of a female in the act of pulling the five strings of a Teutonic cithara or *rotta,* which are fastened to an elongated tail-piece, and rest on a bridge.‡. The Abbot, Martin Gerbert, has published this figure.§ Another *rotta,* of a similar form to the latter, except the bridge, is mounted with seven strings; it is drawn from another manuscript

---

* " Delectat me quoque cytharistam habere, qui possit cytharisare in cithara, quam nos appellamus *Rottae* (sic)."—*Epist.* 89, *ex edit. Serrarii.* [This 89th Letter, it seems, was written by St. Cuthbert.—Tr.]

† Gerbert refers this manuscript to the *sixth* century, thus: *Ex Msc. San-Blas. ann. DC.*—Tr.

‡ M. Fétis appears to have mistaken a portion of the performer's sleeve, shown in perspective, for the " elongated tail-piece" here mentioned.—Tr.

§ *De Cantu et Musica,* vol. ii, Tab. xxvi, fig. 3.

of the ninth century, and an engraving of it has also been given by the Abbot Gerbert*. I know an instrument of the same class—that is, a genuine *rote*, and not a *crouth*, for it has no neck—in a sculpture of the Cathedral of Amiens, which dates from the fifteenth century. From all evidence, the strings of this instrument were pulled; it was a cithara, a *rote*. We see, then, that the erudition of Bottée de Toulmont is in fault, and that the *rote* was not a bow-instrument. M. Coussemaker, true to his system of borrowing, without citing those from whom he copies, has not the conjectural discretion of his predecessor; he adopts the notion without ceremony, and expresses himself categorically in these terms:— " Although chiefly in use among the Britons, the *crout* was of barbarous origin, and has taken the name of *rota* among the poets and romance writers of the middle ages. Many authors have thought that the term *rote* was given to the hurdy-gurdy (*vielle*); but this is erroneous. *Rota* or *rotta* is not derived from *rottare*, but rather from *chrotta*, a German word, of which the sign of aspiration, *ch*, has been suppressed, as in the case of many names of the same origin." † I have merely entered into these details in order to dispel an error which has been accredited among archæologists, who copy from each other, without giving themselves the trouble to verify statements. If the rote is often mentioned by poets and writers before or after bow-instruments, this in no way

---

* *De Cantu et Musica*, vol. ii, Tab. xxxii, fig. 17.

† *Essai sur les instruments de musique du moyen âge*, in the *Annales archéologiques* of Didron, vol. iii, p. 152.

proves that it was an instrument of the same class. As well might we believe that the harp was like the *viol* or the *hurdy-gurdy*, because we find in some old poets passages of the following kind :

> Harpes sonnent et vielles,
> Qui font les mélodies belles.
> (*Romance of Renard*, of the 13th century.)

The text of St. Boniface [Cuthbert] is positive: the rote was a cithara, an instrument whose strings were pulled [by the fingers]. We see also, from a work of a Provençal poet of the twelfth century, that the number of its strings might be increased to seventeen :

> E faits la rota
> A XVII cordas garnir.

Nor can I admit the opinion of the erudite M. Georges Kastner, that the name of *rote* was applied to two instruments of different sorts, one of which was played with the bow, and the other by pulling the strings.* I know not a single text which supports this conjecture.

Let us now return to consider the influence which the *crouth trithant*, or three-stringed crouth, has had in the formation of bow-instruments which were in use on the continent of Europe. M. Hersart de La Villemarqué thought he had traced it in the hands of the Barzou, the mendicant bards of Brittany; for he says : "They accompany themselves with sounds scarcely harmonious, drawn from a musical instrument with three strings, named *rebek*, which is touched with a bow, and

---

* *Les Danses des Morts, dissertations et recherches historiques, philosophiques, littéraires et musicales*, p. 241.

which is no other than the *krouz* or *rote* of the Welsh and British bards of the sixth century."* We perceive, in this passage, the error concerning the rote reproduced after Bottée de Toulmont, and another which belongs to the learned Editor of the *Popular Melodies of Brittany;* namely, the pretended analogy subsisting between the *rebek* of the mendicant poets of the Low Britons and the *crouth* of the Welsh bards. The forms of these instruments are essentially different: for the primitive *crouth* has the body contracted towards the middle, and presents, in its upper and lower parts, equal hemispherical enlargements, or nearly so; whilst the *rebec*, the popular violin of the continent (which is nothing else than the *rubèbe* or *rebelle* of the middle ages, which had at first only one or two strings, like the popular *rébab* of the Arabs),—the *rebec*, I say, was narrowed towards the neck, and gradually enlarged until it rounded off towards the lower end. Its form was that of one of the small varieties of the lute, modified by a tail-piece more or less elongated, a bridge, and a bow to put the strings into vibration. The most ancient representation of an instrument of this kind was extracted by the Abbot Gerbert from a manuscript of the commencement of the ninth century. It has but one string: semicircular sound-holes are cut in the belly, and the string rests on a bridge: a part of the neck appears to be higher than the belly. Here follows a copy of this figure, which shows also a hand directing a bow on the string. (See *Fig.* 3, next page.)

---

* *Barzaz-Breiz, chants populaires de la Bretagne,* introduction, p. xxxiv, 4th edition. Paris, 1846, 2 vols. 12mo.

Fig. 3.

In succeeding centuries, monuments afford us representations of instruments of both kinds; that is to say, either in the form of the *crouth trithant*, more or less modified; or in that which resembles the varieties of the lute. Instruments of this latter species have but two or three strings: if the painter or sculptor gives them four, it is by mistake; for there are many inaccuracies, both in the representations of instruments and the way in which their names are written. The *rubèbe* belongs to this kind, and was only mounted with two strings. Jerome of Moravia, a Dominican of the thirteenth century, informs us that it was a grave-toned instrument, and tuned as follows:*

---

* In chap. xviii of the compilation of different Treatises on Music, the manuscript of which is in the Imperial Library, Paris *(fonds de la Sorbonne*, No. 1817, 4to.)

The acute instrument of the same species was mounted with three strings, and received the name of *gigue*, in France, in the twelfth, thirteenth, and fourteenth centuries; but, in the fifteenth century, this name seems to have been changed for the first time into that of *rebec* for all the instruments of the same family—great, medium, and small. The Germans call them by the name of *Geige ohne Bunde* (viols without bands, i. e. without sides), to distinguish them from other instruments of a more perfect kind.* The following figure shows the form:

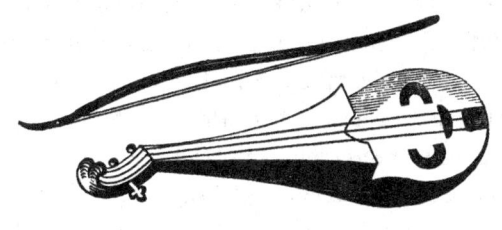

Fig. 4.

The *rubèbe*, the *gigue*—in short, the four classes of the *rebec* kind which we have already found established from the fifteenth century, namely, treble, alto, tenor, and bass, were the popular instruments in the hands of the minstrels, and served in general for dancing and for street singers. Their form was invariably such as we have described. The bass of this species of instrument

---

* See the book of Martin Agricola entitled *Musica instrumentalis.* Wittemberg, 1529), fols. lv and lvi. *Gigue* and *Geige* are evidently the same word in two different languages.

was frequently superseded by the *monochord*, or by the *trumpet marine*, the body of which was a pentagonal cone greatly elongated, on which was set a deal belly or sound-board. The single string of this instrument was tightened by a spring screw (*tourniquet à ressort*) and rested on a bridge, the feet of which were of unequal length. The sounds [which were harmonics] were formed [by lightly pressing the string] with the thumb of the left hand. The bow was greatly curved, and had a large nut which the musician held in his right hand reversed*.

The other class of bow-instruments, which consisted of a sonorous chest formed of a back and belly united by slender ribs, called sides, which were contracted about the middle of their length, like the body of a guitar; this class, I say, the type of which lies in the *crouth trithant* of the sixth century, and which has been designated by the names of *vielle* and *viole* (viol), belongs to a more advanced art ("*ein ander Art*," says Agricola)†. It is thus that, in India, the *sarungies*, the *saroh* and the *chikara*, with four or five gut strings, constructed with much elegance and finish by Gun Pat and Mahamdou, who are the Stradivarius and Guarnerius of Benares, differ essentially from the *ravanastron* and the *omerti*, and belong to a more refined art. It is thus, also, that the *kemángeh roumy* with four or six strings, in use in Persia,

---

* The bow was placed on the string *between the performer and his hand*, instead of between his left hand and the bridge.—TR.

† The necessity for this quotation from Agricola is by no means obvious, as the German word *Art* never signifies that which is understood by this combination of letters in French or English; to express which the word *Kunst* would be used.—TR.

Arabia, Turkey, and Egypt, belongs to music cultivated as an art; whilst the *kemángeh à gouz*, *kemángeh fark*, *kemángeh soghair*, and the *rebab*, each mounted with two strings, are consigned to the people, and require scarcely any study.

From the end of the eleventh century, we notice the *vielles* or *violes* (viols) on monuments. The oldest representations of this kind show us these instruments mounted with four strings. The author of an anonymous treatise on musical instruments which, to all appearance, cannot be later than the thirteenth century*, attributes the invention of the viol with four strings to a certain Albinus, and gives a very imperfect drawing of it. The term *invention* can only be taken for *modification*. At what period did this Albinus flourish? † We know not; but, in the work in question, we find a valuable indication of the tuning of the four strings, which are represented by the letters *a*, *d*, *g*, *c*, corresponding with the notes:

This tuning by fourths is met with in the viols of the sixteenth century; but it has varied, as we shall presently see.

---

* *De diversis monochordis, tetrachordis, pentachordis, exachordis, eptachordis, octochordis, &c. ex quibus diversa formantur instrumenta musicæ, cum figuris instrumentorum.* This treatise is found in a manuscript collection of different works on music, preserved in the Library of the University of Gand, No. 171.

† Mr. William Chappell says, in his *Popular Music of the Olden Time*, vol. ii, p. 763, there can be very little doubt that the Albinus here referred to was Alcuin, who died in 804, and who assumed the name of Flaccus Albinus in his writings.—Tr.

Many viols of the thirteenth century have five strings, according to the monuments which exhibit them: so, likewise, have those of which Jerome of Moravia speaks, in the work before mentioned. The form of these instruments is always that of the guitar; which form is steadily preserved throughout the fourteenth century. The absence of the bridge is the most remarkable peculiarity of these figures, which invariably appear under this shape:

Fig. 5.

In a great many figures of viols or vielles which we meet with on monuments, in manuscripts, and even in works of a date approaching our own time—such as those of Martin Agricola* and of Othmar Lucinius or Nachtgall †—we observe that some have bridges, and others have not, even at the same periods. Thus,

---

* *Musica instrumentalis deutsch, &c.* printed at Wittemberg, by George Rhaw, 1529, sm. 8vo.

† *Musurgia seu Praxis musicæ. Illius primo quæ instrumentis agitur certa ratio, &c.* Argentorati, apud Johannem Schottum, 1536, sm. obl. 4to.

on the ancient gateway of the Abbey of St. Denis, which was constructed in the twelfth century, three figures represent viols with five strings and with three, which have bridges. The gateway of Notre Dame of Chartres, which is also of the twelfth century, displays among its sculptures a vielle with three strings, with a bridge. On the contrary, a rubèbe with two strings, in the hands of an angel, in the window of the Abbey of Bon-Port, in Normandy, and belonging to the thirteenth century, has no bridge.

A viol with five strings, which occurs in a French romance of the fourteenth century (MS. No. 6737 of the Imperial Library, Paris), has a bridge; but a rebec with three strings, shown in the *Miroir historial* of Vincent of Beauvais (MSS. of the fifteenth century, No. 6731 of the same library), and a little viol, also with three strings, which is found in a manuscript of the *Bible historiaux*, of the same period (No. 6819 of the same library), have not any.

A large viol with four strings, which a woman holds between her legs, in the book entitled *les Échecs amoureux* (MSS. of the fifteenth century, No. 6808 of the Imp. Lib.), has a bridge. The same is the case with a little rebec with three strings, held by a siren, in the same volume. This rebec has the precise form of those which are represented in the work of Martin Agricola[*]. Lastly, we see a bridge on a viol with four strings in the book of *Proverbes et Adages* of the sixteenth century (MSS. No. 4316 fonds de la Vallière, in the same

---

[*] *Musica instrum. &c.* pp. lv, lvi.

library). However, at the same period, two well-informed men—Othmar Nachtgall and Martin Agricola—who have specially treated the matter in question, have represented, in their works, viols whose strings are fastened to a tail-piece similar to that of a guitar, and without a bridge, as in this figure:

Fig. 6.

Now, it would have been absolutely impossible to prevent the bow touching all the strings at once of an instrument so made. Besides, the sounds which we might attempt to draw from it would be extremely weak; for it is the bridge which gives the requisite angle to the strings to enable them to vibrate with *éclat*, and to communicate their motion to the sound-board; in short, it is the bridge which, vibrating energetically itself, imparts to the sound-board, by its precipitate beatings, the vibratory oscillations from whence intensity of sound results. Moreover, we must not forget that the principle of the production of sounds, by the friction of the bow on the strings, was accompanied, from its very origin, by the necessary appendage of the bridge. We find it in the primitive essay of the *ravanastron*, and in the *omerti*, of India; in the *rebab*, and in the *kemángeh à gouz*, of the Arabs; in short, wherever the bow is met with. It is, then, beyond doubt that the absence of the bridge in some monuments of the middle ages, and in the figures published by Agricola and by Othmar Nachtgall, is purely attributable to the inadvertence or the forgetfulness of the designers. Of this we have a proof, in regard to what is seen in these two authors themselves; for their contemporary, Silvestro Ganassi del Fontego, from whom we have a special treatise on the art of playing the viol*, has represented a concert, in the frontispiece of his book, in which the viols have bridges.

Two new facts of great importance are revealed in the figures published by Agricola, Nachtgall, and Ganassi del Fontego; namely: the bends or hollows which have replaced the slightly defined curves on the sides of the instruments, and the frets which occur on the necks of viols, like those which are still seen on guitars. The figures represent these bends inaccurately, for they are too greatly extended, and consequently the upper and lower parts of the instruments are reduced to too small proportions. Some viols and bass viols of the sixteenth century, which still exist in the cabinets of the curious, demonstrate that the bends were of less extent, although proportionally greater than in violins, altos, and violoncellos.

Want of skill in the performers induced the putting of frets on the neck of the instruments, in order to show the places where the fingers should be set to produce the desired notes: so that, instead of being instruments of variable sounds, and adapted for perfect intonation, the

---

* *Regola Rubertina che insegna a sonar de viola d'archo tastada da Silvestro Ganasi* (sic) *del Fontego*. In Venetia, ad instantia de l'autore, 1542, sm. obl. 4to.

viols became instruments of fixed sounds and tempered. This usage was continued to the first half of the eighteenth century, although the violin had been freed from these shackles nearly one hundred and fifty years.

There was evidently a great variety in the construction of viols, at the period when true music began to appear and harmony became more refined. This change took place towards the end of the fourteenth century, by the happy efforts of three musicians, superior to their time: Dufay, Binchois, and Dunstaple*. The whole range of the art was then comprised in the harmony produced by the union of the different species of voices. That which applied to voices, therefore, it was desired to make applicable to instruments; and as there are acute voices, called *soprano*, less acute, termed *contralto*, medium voices, or *tenors*, and grave, called *basses*, the idea was conceived of making, in all kinds of instruments, complete families which should represent these four species of voices. Thus, viols, hautboys, flutes, cornets, &c. had their soprano, alto, tenor, and bass, and sometimes even their double bass. This division, which became established in the fifteenth century, was maintained during the sixteenth and seventeenth, or rather has not ceased up to the present time, at least for bow-instruments. The most common instruments had their quartett, complete: thus we see, in the work of Agricola, the treble, alto, tenor, and bass of the *rebec*, each mounted with three strings, with a triangular bridge, the summit of which supported the middle string,

---

* *Dunstable* appears to be the preferable orthography.—Tr.

in order that the bow might not touch all three strings at once.

Singular variations are observable in the form and dimensions of viols, and in the manner of stringing them, from the first half of the sixteenth century. The book of Agricola, printed in 1529, exhibits a complete quartett of little viols, with heads turned back, like those of lutes, and mounted with three strings only. Agricola designates them by the name of *kleine Geigen mit Bünden und mit dreien Seyten* (little viols with sides and with three strings). Like all instruments of the same species, their neck is divided by six frets*, Michael Prætorius says, indeed, in his *Organographia*, printed in 1619 †, that viols with three strings were used in ancient times, and that there were others with four and with five strings. Agricola gives the figures of the quartett of viols with four strings ‡, the details of construction of which are similar to those of the viols with three strings. The following are the tunings of the instruments which compose the quartett:

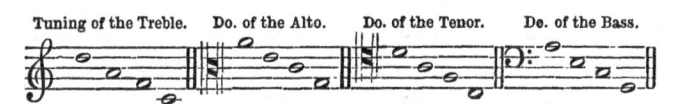

Tuning of the Treble.   Do. of the Alto.   Do. of the Tenor.   Do. of the Bass.

Lastly, the great viols, with five strings, which Agricola mentions, formed a quartett, like the others;

---

* *Musica instrumentalis*, pp. li, lii.
† *Syntagma Musicum*, vol. ii, p. 45.
‡ *Loc. cit.* p. xlvi, verso.

with this difference, however, that the bass was mounted with six strings. They were tuned as follows:

Tuning of the Treble. Do. of the Alto and Tenor. Do. of the Bass.

But even at the time when bow-instruments of the viol species were classed, strung, and tuned, in Germany, in the manner described above, the viols of Italy presented remarkable differences, as we see in the valuable book of Ganassi del Fontego, on the art of playing these instruments. The Italian viols were mounted with six strings; they had seven frets on the finger-board, by means of which the neck of each viol was divided into a chromatic scale of two octaves and a half. Their tunings were as follow:

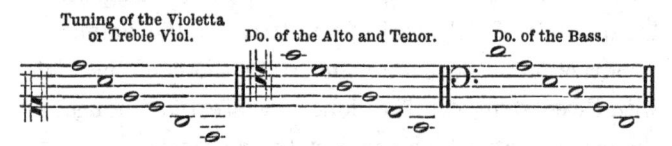

Tuning of the Violetta or Treble Viol. Do. of the Alto and Tenor. Do. of the Bass.

Sometimes the alto differed from the tenor, in that it was tuned a fifth above the bass. We must remark that this mode of tuning bow-instruments by two fourths in descending, followed by a third, and this again by two fourths, is precisely that of the lute and its varieties. It is evident that from that period—namely, from the first half of the sixteenth century—the art adapted itself to a regular system. We find the same tuning in 1601, in the musical treatise by Cerreto*; and still the same

---

* *Della Prattica musica vocale et strumentale*, lib. iv, p. 331.

is presented to us by Mersenne, in his *Harmonie universelle*, in 1636*.

However, if we turn again to Germany, in the first half of the seventeenth century, we there find differences in the viol which deserve to fix our attention for a moment. Michael Prætorius, a great musician, and a composer of rare skill, who also was learned both in the history and in the theory of his art, produced a great treatise on music, the second volume of which is entirely devoted to the instruments of his time and those of former periods†. Now, from this work we learn that the quartett of the *viola di gamba* (leg viol), as the Germans have called it since that time, or rather the quintett (for there are double bass viols),—from this work, I say, we learn that these instruments had larger proportions, and that they were tuned lower. We learn also that the *violetta* or soprano [viol], was mounted with three, four, five, or six strings, according to circumstances; that the alto had but three or four strings; the tenor, five or six; the bass, three, four, or six; and the double bass, five or six. In short, we learn that, when these instruments had six strings (with the exception of the alto), their tuning was as follows:

---

* *Traité des Instruments à chordes*, liv. IV, p. 194.
† *Syntagmatis musici, tomus secundus. De Organographia*, p. 25.

Thus, as we see, these instruments are all tuned a fourth lower than the Italian viols. At such a pitch, they could only produce a dull and mournful effect. They were all played on the knee, except the bass, which was held between the legs, and the double bass, which was played standing.

There was another viol, whose sides were narrower than those of the bass viol, and which was called *viola bastarda* (bastard viol), because it was tuned by fifths and fourths.

We have now approached towards the end of the sixteenth century, and, up to this period, have found nothing in the form of the violin, although the name of *violino* had already occurred in a work of Giovanni Maria Lanfranco, printed at Brescia in 1533*. Does he speak of the *violin* such as we know in the present day; or merely of the little viol, which was called, somewhat later, *violetta?* This is difficult to determine. The first precise reference [to the violin], although given in an indirect way and without the least detail, is found in the first part of the *Prattica di Musica*, by Ludovico Zacconi, printed at Venice in 1596. He there gives the compass of various instruments of his time, and among them that of the violin, represented in this manner : †

---

* *Scintille, ossia regole di musica, che mostrano a leggere il canto firmo e figurato, gli accidenti delle note mensurate, le proportioni e tuoni, il contrapunto e la divisione d'il monocordo ; con la accordatura di varii instrumenti, &c.* cap. ultimo.

† Lib. iv, p. 218 verso.

This is, indeed, the real compass of the violin, from the fourth open string of the instrument to the use of the fourth finger on the first string; because the *shift* was then, and even for a considerable time afterwards, wholly unknown. Now, this compass does not agree with that of any viol known. However, although the violin evidently existed from that time, it was doubtless but little used in Italy; for its name does not appear in the enumeration and analysis of the instruments given by Cerreto in his book printed in 1601*. The first certain use of the violin occurs in Monteverde's *Orfeo*, which was performed at Mantua in 1607†; but even the author's own words lead us to believe that this modification of the viol did not originate in Italy : for, in the enumeration of his orchestra, which precedes the introductory symphony, he mentions—besides ten *viole da brazzo* (arm viols), three *bassi da gamba* (leg basses), and two *contra-bassi di viola* (double bass viols)—*duoi violini piccoli alla francese* (two little violins of the French sort). However this may be, we find the violin soon afterwards, in the form now known, in the *Theatrum Instrumentorum, seu Sciagraphia*, of Michael Prætorius, published at Wolfenbuttel in 1620. The curves [in the sides], the corners and the purfling, are all like those of our violin. Sound-holes of the *ƒƒ* shape have been substituted for those made like ↃC ; the neck, free (*dégagé*), narrow and rounded, has there taken the place of the broad, flat

---

* Lib. iv, cap. viii—xi, pp. 313—335.

† *L'Orfeo, favola in musica da Claudio Monteverde, maestro di capella della serenissima republica* (di Venezia), *rappresentato in Mantova l'anno* 1607. Venice, 1615. 2nd edition.

neck of the viol; the finger-board is disencumbered from frets. The bridge alone is still plain, and cut out only in the lower part, which forms the feet*. Already the system is complete; for we there find the *quint* or alto, the violoncello, and the great *quint bass*, or double bass. The tuning of the violin is E, A, D, G; that of the alto, A, D, G, C; that of the violoncello, like that of the alto, an octave lower; and, lastly, that of the *quint bass*, which is mounted with five strings, is:

Such is the sketch of the history of bow-instruments, confined to the most essential details, prior to the time when the great Italian school so admirably illustrated it. We have now to trace the relation between the makers belonging to this school, who have contributed to the progress and transformations in the manufacture of these instruments, until their highest perfection was attained by the renowned master who is the subject of this notice.

---

* See the *Sciagraphia* of Prætorius, pl. xx, figs. 4 and 5.
† *Syntagm. music.* vol. ii, p. 26.

VIOLIN MAKERS OF THE ITALIAN SCHOOLS

FROM THE EARLIEST TIMES.

THE fifteenth century reveals to us but a single name, and even that is a subject of doubt. According to Laborde, there was in Brittany, about 1450, a stringed-instrument maker named *Kerlin*, of whose workmanship he had seen a violin, made in 1449. In 1804, that is, about twenty-five years after the date when Laborde wrote, this instrument was found in the possession of Koliker, a violin maker at Paris; at which time we saw it. However, it was not a violin, but a viol, whose neck had been changed, and which was mounted with four strings, like a violin. The instrument bulged more than the viols of a later period, and the rise* of its back and belly was very great. Its upper and lower extremities were not accurately rounded, and the corners were blunt and curtailed. Instead of the ordinary tail-piece, there was an ivory attachment pierced with four holes for fastening the strings, which seemed to indicate that this instrument belonged to the

---

* By the *rise*, *swell*, or *arching* of the back and belly of violins and other stringed instruments, is to be understood the degree of elevation of those parts, viewed longitudinally.—TR.

species of *Geige* with four strings, which is mentioned in the work of Martin Agricola. The quality of tone was sweet and subdued. The instrument bore within it this inscription: *Joan. Kerlino, ann.* 1449. This name, commencing with the syllable *Ker*, probably led Laborde to believe that the maker flourished in Brittany; because the names of many families in that country are known to begin in the same way; but from information recently obtained from Italy—through a correspondent of M. Vuillaume, who has long dealt in bow-instruments, and had numerous originals pass through his hands— we learn that there was a maker at Brescia, about 1450, named *John Kerlino*. There is every reason to believe that the instrument possessed by Koliker, at the beginning of this century, was made by this artist, and that he was the founder of the school of Brescia, one of the oldest and most distinguished in Italy. It is worthy of remark that Kerlino, like all the makers of the first period whose names and works are known, made only rebecs, viols of all dimensions, *lire d'arco* and *lirone* with eleven and twelve strings.

After Kerlino, the oldest Italian maker is Pietro Dardelli, of Mantua, who flourished about the year 1500, and of whose manufacture some beautiful viols still exist in the cabinets of the curious. Then came Gaspard Duiffoprugcar, a celebrated artist, born in the Italian Tyrol, and who established himself in Bologna, about 1510. Fine instruments of this maker, such as bass-viols, tenors, and *violettas*, or little viols, constructed by Duiffoprugcar for the chapel and the chamber of Francis the First, King of France, have been preserved by different amateurs in Paris until the present time. A superb bass-viol, on the back of which is represented the plan of Paris in the fifteenth century, is now the property of M. Vuillaume, but previously belonged to the late J. M. Raoul, King's Counsellor, and Advocate in the Court of Cassation. This amateur—a violoncellist of some merit, who has published several compositions and a Method for the Violoncello— endeavoured to resuscitate the bass-viol, to which he gave the name of *heptachord*. A notice on the labours of M. Raoul on this subject has appeared in the *Revue Musicale* by the author of this work (tome ii, pp. 56—61).

In gradually approaching the middle of the sixteenth century, we find Venturi Linarolli, who worked at Venice in 1520; Peregrino Zanetto, of Brescia, in 1540; and Morglato Morella, of Mantua, perhaps a pupil of Dardelli, and of whom instruments are known bearing the date 1550. It thus appears that these old masters made nothing but viols of all kinds and sizes, most of which have been destroyed to form tenor violins, and to repair ancient instruments which are still in use. Modern violin makers have always sought after them for this purpose.

The first period of Italian viol-making, of which we have just spoken, was succeeded by that of the creation of the violin, and its relatives of deeper pitch—the alto, the violoncello, the bass (of somewhat larger dimensions than the preceding), and the quint-bass, or primitive double-bass. The first in date, among the artists of this second period, is Gaspard or Gasparo di Salo, so called because he was born in the little town of Salo, on the lake of Garda, in Lombardy. He was one of the best Italian makers of the sixteenth century, and worked at Brescia from 1560 to about 1610, that is to say, for nearly fifty years; instruments of his manufacture having been found with these distant dates. Gasparo di Salo was particularly renowned for his viols, bass-viols and *violoni*, or double-bass viols; besides which, some violins of his make are known, which are distinguished for their fine quality of tone. Of these, there was one very remarkable instrument, bearing the date 1566, in a valuable collection which was sold at Milan in 1807. Baron de Bagge also possessed one about the year 1788, of which Rudolph Kreutzer spoke with admiration. Mr. T. Forster, an English amateur, and the owner of a numerous collection of violins, has one which bears within it the inscription: *Gasparo di Salo in Brescia*, 1613. Its quality of tone is clear, but dry. If this instrument is genuine, it is a degenerate production of the maker's old age.

A little later, John Paul Magini, born in Brescia, worked in his native town from 1590 to about 1640, and was perhaps a pupil of the artist just named. He especially distinguished himself in the manufacture of violins. The pattern of his instruments is, in general, large; their proportions are the same as those of Gasparo di Salo, and the style of workmanship is similar. The swell, or arching, is decided, and reaches almost to the edges. The sides, or ribs, are narrow; the bellies, very strong, and of good quality; the backs, generally thin, with the wood cut on the layers (*sur couche*).* The varnish, which is remarkable for its delicacy, is of a yellowish light brown colour, and of excellent quality. The extended dimensions, and the proportion of the arching relative to that of the thickness, impart to most of these instruments a superb, grave, and melancholy tone.

Before Gasparo di Salo, there was nothing definitively settled as regards the form of the violin; but it is quite evident, from his productions, that henceforth the existing shape of this instrument became firmly established. Subsequently, the differences of detail among the instruments of various makers are so slight, that they are only obvious to a well-practised eye.

A cotemporary of John Paul Magini, Anthony Mariani, of Pesaro, likewise manufactured violins from 1570 to about 1620; but his instruments, made at random, and without fixed principles, have no value, and are not even sought after as objects of curiosity.

---

* In examining the transverse section of the trunk of a tree which has been felled for some time, two marked features will be observed; namely: 1st, the clearly defined circles which, gradually enlarging, surround the heart of the tree, and which represent the annual layers or growths of the wood; and, 2ndly, the cracks or fissures caused by the dessication of the timber, and which extend in straight lines from the centre towards the circumference. These cracks are termed, in French, *mailles*, and planks which are sawn in the direction of them—that is, from the heart to the bark—are said to be cut *sur maille;* while those which are sawn as nearly as possible on the annual layers above described, are said to be cut *sur couche*. In England, different terms are used by the sawyers in different counties to designate these modes of cutting the timber. *On the quarter* seems to be one of the most usual for that answering to the French *sur maille;* and for the other (*sur couche*) we have adopted the expression *on the layers*, in order to render the meaning perfectly intelligible to the reader, who, in addition, will invariably find the French terms given in a parenthesis.—Tr.

But such is not the case with those of Magini. In the first few years of this century, they were little known in France; but the celebrated violinist, De Beriot, fixed the attention of artists on their merits, and established their reputation by the success which he achieved, both in Paris and in London, on an instrument of this master.

We must not confound John Paul Magini with another maker of Brescia, probably of the same family, who flourished in the seventeenth century, and was named Santo Magini. Although violins of his make exist, he is more particularly distinguished for his double-basses, which are renowned in Italy as the best instruments of this class.

About the year 1580, the school of Brescia also produced two other artists of merit, although of an inferior order to John Paul Magini. The first was Javietta Budiani, and the other, Matteo Bente. The instruments of the latter are much sought after by those who form collections.

We now come to the head of a family, illustrious in the manufacture of musical instruments, who was also founder of the great school of Cremona. Andrew Amati was descended from an ancient decurional family of that town, which is mentioned in the Cremonese annals of 1097. The date of his birth is unknown, as the registers of the churches of Cremona do not go back to the commencement of the sixteenth century, the period when his birth appears to have happened; but, in default of a baptismal record, we have positive information touching this artist, furnished by a violin or rebec with three strings, which existed in the valuable collection of instruments formed by Count Cozio de Salabue, of Casal-Monferrato, and preserved at Milan, at the residence of the Chevalier Carlo Carli. This instrument bore the name of Andrew Amati, and the date of 1546. Baron de Bagge possessed, also, about 1788, a medium viol *(viole moyenne)*, otherwise called, in Italy, *viola bastarda*, which bore the date 1551. It is therefore certain that Andrew Amati was born during the first twenty years of the sixteenth century.

Who was the master of Andrew? Where did he acquire the skill which is observable in his works? We know not. The author of a letter inserted in the " *Correspondence of Professors and Amateurs of Music*," published by Cockatrix, in 1803, assures us that Andrew Amati worked as an apprentice at Brescia, before establishing a shop of his own at Cremona. The fact is not impossible, for the two towns are situated near each other, in Lombardy; but assertions of this kind are of no value unless supported by documentary evidence of incontestible authority. The instruments of Andrew Amati have particular forms, which clearly distinguish them from those of the ancient school of Brescia. He must have made special studies before adopting the proportions answering to the requirements of his time. When he worked, no one demanded a tone of that power and brilliance which is now required. So far from it, an instrument which should have possessed such a degree of sonority would have offended the ears of an audience accustomed to the tranquil music of which we still possess specimens. The spinets, lutes, theorbos, mandoras, and guitars—all these instruments, which were used in their public and private concerts (for, indeed, they had no others)—all these, we repeat, had but little power. What was demanded of a maker at that period, was, that his instruments should possess a sweet and mellow tone. Now, in justice to the head of the Amati family, it must be admitted that his violins, viols, and basses leave nothing to desire in this respect.

Andrew Amati made many instruments; but time has impaired and accidents have destroyed a great number of them. Before the first French revolution (1789), there existed among the valuable properties belonging to the Chapel Royal, a collection of violins and viols which had been made by Andrew Amati by order of Charles the Ninth, an enthusiastic amateur of music. After the days of the 5th and 6th of October, 1790, all these instruments disappeared from Versailles. Cartier (see this name in the *Biographie universelle des Musiciens*) discovered two of the violins many years after these events. Their sonority lacked brilliance; but the quality of their tone was charming, and the workmanship remarkable for its finish.

The violins of Andrew Amati are of small and medium pattern, and their swell or arching is very decided towards the centre. The wood of the back is cut on the layers *(sur couche)*; the bellies, of a good quality, are sufficiently thick; and the varnish is substantial, and of a light brown colour. As before observed, their intensity of sound is relative to the period when they were made.

The date of Andrew Amati's death is unknown; but

it probably occurred about 1580: because the instruments marked with the name of Amati, after this period, belong to his sons, Jerome and Anthony. The latter, born at Cremona about 1550, succeeded his father, and after being some time associated with Jerome, he ultimately separated from him.

Anthony adopted the patterns of Andrew; but he made a much greater number of small, than of large, violins. Those of the latter kind which have emanated from the associated brothers are much esteemed, and greatly sought for, if in a good state of preservation. The violinist Libon possessed an admirable one of them, of a delightful quality of tone, on which he performed the quartetts of Haydn, about 1809, with Messrs. de Sermentôt, de Noailles, and de Villeblanche, enthusiastic amateurs, at whose abodes were heard the most eminent artists of the period. The violin of Libon, made by Anthony and Jerome Amati, bore the date of 1591. The small violins made by Anthony Amati have a sweet and mellow tone, which, although very pure, has, unfortunately, but little intensity. The first and second strings are the best parts of these instruments; the third is somewhat dull; and the fourth, too feeble. In the good instruments of the two brothers, the workmanship is of exquisite finish. The well-selected wood is cut on the layers (*sur couche*) for the back and the sides; the deal used for the bellies has a fine and delicate grain; the swell or arching is high in the centre, and the breasts are very sloping, *(les gorges sont très-évidées)*. The pro-proportions of thickness combined with the other conditions found in these instruments give them that fine, delicate, and sweet tone which is their distinctive quality. Anthony Amati died, it is supposed, in 1635; at all events, it is certain that his name does not appear upon any instrument posterior to that date.

After working a long time with his brother, Jerome Amati married; which change of condition induced the two brothers to separate. From that time, Jerome no longer adhered to the exact reproduction of the models of Andrew; for some violins of his are known which are of a larger pattern than those of Anthony or of the old Amati. Jerome, after his separation, occasionally approached his brother in finish; but, on the whole, he is inferior to him. He died in 1638.

Among the number of pupils of Anthony and Jerome Amati must be mentioned Gioacchino or Giòfredo Cappa, who was born at Cremona in 1590. In 1640 he established himself at Piedmont, and there formed the school of violin makers of Saluzzo, where the reigning Prince then dwelt. He there made a great number of instruments, and formed good pupils, among whom were Acevo and Sapino, whose productions, without equalling those of the Amati, were formerly esteemed. The violoncellos of Cappa are his best instruments.

Nicholas Amati, the son of Jerome, who is justly regarded as the most celebrated of the artists of that name, was born on the 3rd of September, 1596, and died on the 12th of August, 1684, at the age of eighty-eight, according to the registers of the Cathedral of Cremona. He made but little change in the forms and proportions adopted by his family, but gave a higher finish to details, with greater perfection in the design of the curves, and produced a varnish more supple and mellow, and possessing a superior appearance. The proportions of the arching and of the thickness of his instruments are better calculated than in those of either Andrew, Anthony, or Jerome. Hence, it follows that, while preserving their distinctive sweetness of tone, they have greater power and brilliance. Some violins on which this celebrated maker would appear to have worked with partiality are veritable masterpieces of his art. One of them, bearing the date 1668, existed at Milan, in the collection of Count Cozio de Salabue. In perfection of finish, and purity and mellowness of tone, this instrument was considered a marvel of its kind. The Count de Castelbarco, of the same city, also possesses some which are admirable; and that belonging to the celebrated violinist Allard is cited as one of the best instruments ever made by Nicholas Amati.

Nicholas had two sons, by his wife Lucretia Pagliari, of whom the elder, Jerome, was born the 26th of February, 1649, and the other, John Baptist, born the 13th of August, 1657, became a priest and died about 1706. Jerome worked in his father's shop, and succeeded him. He slightly enlarged the pattern of his violins, but was much less pains-taking than the other members of his family, and very inferior to his father: he also produced but few instruments. One violin of his is known, dated 1672: it is one of his latest works. This Jerome was the last artist of the name of Amati.

The pupils formed by Nicholas Amati, are: his son Jerome, Andrew Guarnerius, Paolo Grancino, who settled at Milan and worked there from 1665 to 1690, and the illustrious ANTHONY STRADIVARI or STRADIVARIUS, of Cremona, an account of whom forms the grand object of the present publication.

The following chronological list contains the names of those makers who are generally considered as belonging to the Amati school, either because they had worked with Jerome, the son of Nicholas, or had been formed by the pupils of this school and had followed its traditions with greater or less exactness.

THE AMATI SCHOOL.

	Flourished.
Joseph Guarnerius, son of Andrew, of Cremona	from 1680 to 1710
Florinus Florentus, of Bologna	from 1685 to 1715
Francis Rugger (or Ruggieri), surnamed *il Per*, of Cremona	from 1670 to 1720
Peter Guarnerius, brother of Joseph and second son of Andrew	from 1690 to 1720
John Grancino, son of Paolo, of Milan	from 1696 to 1720
John Baptist Grancino, brother of John, of Milan	from 1690 to 1700
Alexander Mezzadie, of Ferrara	from 1690 to 1720
Dominicelli, of Ferrara	from 1695 to 1715
Vincent Rugger, of Cremona	from 1700 to 1730
John Baptist Rugger, of Brescia	from 1700 to 1725
Peter James Rugger, of Brescia	from 1700 to 1720
Gaetano Pasta, of Brescia	from 1710 to ....
Domenico Pasta, of Brescia	from 1710 to ....
Francis Grancino, son of John, and grandson of Paolo, of Milan	from 1710 to 1746
Peter Guarnerius, son of Joseph, and grandson of Andrew, of Cremona	from 1725 to 1740
Santo Serafino, of Venice	from 1730 to 1745

The labours of Gaspard di Salo, John Paul Magini, and the Amati established the present form of the violin, invented in the sixteenth century, and suddenly carried to a state of perfection that is not one of the least astonishing facts in this century so teeming with wonders. If we compare this instrument with one of those viols whose use was retained in France to the time of Rameau (1750)—and which are commonly known by the name of *quintons*—we shall find it difficult to conceive that, from a thing so imperfect, there arose, from the first attempt, an instrument whose form we have in vain endeavoured to modify in latter times; and from which we have neither been able to take, nor to it to add, anything, without causing deterioration.

In short, there is nothing more admirable than the acoustical relations of the violin : in proof of which, it will suffice to give a simple account of its construction. Its body, the length of which is from 35 to 36 centimètres [13.779 to 14.173 in.], has a breadth of 21 centimètres [8.268 in.] in its widest, and of 11 centimètres [4.331 in.] in its narrowest, part. Its greatest thickness does not exceed 6 centimètres [2.362 in.]. Its sides are so thin that the weight of the body of the instrument is not more than about 240 grammes [about 8½ oz. avoirdupois]; yet, this machine, so frail in appearance, presents a surprisingly energetic resistance to the causes of destruction which continually act upon it; for the violin has supported during centuries a tension of from 40 to 42 kilogrammes [from about 88 to 92 lbs.], and a pressure of 12 kilogrammes [about 26½ lbs] on its weakest part. Its symmetrical figure—its graceful contour and fine proportions—its corresponding bends situated in the middle of its length—the arched surfaces of its back and belly, consolidated by the bar and sound post—the four triangular supports within the corners of the bends, and the two blocks placed at each end—all these are so harmoniously adjusted, that the resistance and the elasticity [of the structure] are in a state of perfect equilibrium.

The bends in the sides of the instrument are not merely designed to enable the bow to act freely on the four strings, for they exercise also a very happy influence on the force and brilliance of the sound; in that the extremities of the instrument produce energetic vibrations which are reflected back again to the place from whence the impulse proceeded. This is what Chanot did not understand when he desired to do away with the bends together with their angles, thinking thereby to introduce the most valuable innovation for augmenting the sonority of the violin, while he simply reproduced the form of the viols of the middle ages.

In the conformation of the violin, everything has been anticipated, not only for the production of its sounds, but also for ensuring its solidity, its preservation, and for remedying unforeseen accidents. For instance, it was requisite there should be a means of getting at the inside, in order to effect indispensable repairs. To attain this object, the ingenious idea was conceived of making the back and belly sufficiently wide that their edges might extend about 2 millimètres [.079 in.] beyond the sides; this on the one hand serves as a point of support for the tool used for unglueing them, and on the other it leaves no traces of the operation of re-glueing. Besides, these edges are relieved and ornamented with a large purfling of three colours, presenting an outline of the instrument and, indeed, performing the office of a hem destined to preserve the fragility of the back and belly. Nothing like this existed in the viols which immediately preceded the violin.

It would be a great mistake to suppose that the position and form of the f-holes, which, in the violin, alto, and bass, replace the openings of the older instruments, are arbitrary. The position of these f-holes, their form, the minutest details of their cutting, are such essential points, that no alteration whatever can be made in them without injuring the quality of the tone.

The neck of the violin is no less entitled to praise than the other parts of the instrument, from the simplicity of its disposition and its graceful outline, so happily terminated by the elegance of the scroll. Lastly, the apparatus which serves to distend the strings (the putting into vibration of which reveals the qualities of the instrument) is the simplest and the best-conceived which it is possible to imagine.

Maple and deal are the constituent elements of the violin; which woods present infinite varieties, by reason of the different countries which produce them, and the climates under which their growth is developed. The maple used by the old Italian makers came from Croatia, Dalmatia, and even from Turkey. It was sent to Venice, prepared for oars used for the galleys; and the Turks, it is said, always in rivalry and often at war with the

Venetians, took care to select wood with the greatest number of waves in it, in order that it might break the sooner. It is from these parts of the wood intended for the rowers that the Italian makers chose what suited them for the manufacture of violins.

The deal employed by the Cremona makers was selected from the southern side of the mountains of Italian Switzerland and the Tyrol. Stradivarius, of whom we speak, generally chose those parts of it in which the fibres were small, straight, slightly separated, and always placed perpendicularly to the plane of the violin.

We have now related what were the results of the labours of the great makers of the school of Brescia, and of the Amati family. In the instruments of Gasparo di Salo and Magini we find a tone at once superb, majestic, and penetrating, but veiled and melancholy; in those of Nicholas, the most able of the Amati, a pure, sweet and silvery tone, but little intensity. Mellowness and beauty united to clearness, brilliance and vibratory power—this was the last problem to resolve. A man at length appeared, who, by progressive steps, ultimately discovered the secret of all these perfections combined. This man was Anthony Stradivarius, of whom we are about to speak. After relating all that it has been possible to collect concerning his person and family, we shall follow him in his labours, and shall set forth, beyond doubt and discussion (at least, we hope so), the principles which have resulted from his studies, and which have guided him in the finest productions of his talent.

ANTHONY STRADIVARIUS.

IMPROVEMENTS OF BOW-INSTRUMENTS.

ANTHONY STRADIVARI, born at Cremona, was descended from a very ancient decurional and senatorial family of that city. In the catalogue of ancient families who have filled public offices, which is preserved in the municipal archives of Cremona, we find a succession of members of this family who have been invested with the highest dignities, from 1127 to 1474. In 1127, Ottolinus Stradivarius was *senator patriæ*. In 1186, Egidius Stradivarius bore the same title. In a manuscript volume, existing in the same archives, and entitled *Inscriptiones Cremonenses Universæ*, occurs the epitaph of the latter (p. ccx, No. 1512), copied from the sepulchral inscription which exists in the Church of St. Laurence of the Olivite Fathers: it runs thus—

Egidius. Stradivarius. Patriæ suæ. Crem. senator
Summa. in Omnes. Munific. Liberalitate. Er.
Hic. Corpus. suum. Jacet
Obiit an. Hum. sal. 1199. 4 Id. apr.
Laura. Schitia. uxor. Cariss. P.

The same collection also gives the copy (p. lxiii, No. 378) of the epitaph of Guglielmus Stradivertus, an excellent lawyer, who died in 1439. This inscription exists in the suppressed Church of St. Andrew, at Cremona, and is as follows:

Hodie. Mihi. Cras. Tibi
Viator
Respice. Finem
Guglielmus. Stradivertus
J. C. Præstantissimus
Sibi. suisque. Æredibus
Hic. Situs. Est
Obiit. Anno. MCCCCXXXIX.

We perceive, from the registers above mentioned, that the Stradivari family was sometimes called *Stradivarius*, sometimes *Stradivera*, and even *Stradiverta*.

Notwithstanding the perseverance of M. Vuillaume, in his researches to discover the precise date of the birth of Stradivarius, and despite the devoted complaisance of M. Julius Fusetti, vicar of the Cathedral of Cremona, who has spared no pains in order to attain this object, through circumstances which it is impossible to explain, this date cannot be found. It is therefore presumable that, at the time of the suppression of many of the churches of Cremona, their archives may have been stolen, concealed, or even destroyed. Fortunately, however, one memorial remains, which dispels all doubt as to the *year* when the celebrated violin maker came into the world. Among the memoranda of Carlo Carli, banker at Milan, occurs an inventory of the instruments which belonged to Count Cozio de Salabue, and which were deposited with him. Now, in this inventory, appears a violin of Stradivarius, having within it a label written by the hand of the maker himself, and in which we read his name, his age (ninety-two years), and the date 1736. Stradivarius was therefore born in the year 1644.

As a pupil of Nicholas Amati, he manufactured, in 1667—that is, at the age of twenty-three years—some violins which were merely the exact reproduction of the forms of his master, and in which he placed the label of Nicholas. It was not until 1670 that he began to sign his instruments with his own name. In the twenty years following, to 1690, he produced but few. We are inclined to think that the artist was then more occupied in meditations and experiments on his art, than on labours in a commercial point of view. In the disposition of the wood, cut on the layers (*sur couche*), in the pattern, in the arching and in the varnish, the instruments then made by Stradivarius are but little different from those of Nicholas Amati.

The year 1690 is a very marked period of transition in the career of Anthony Stradivarius. It was then that he began to give greater amplitude to his model, to improve the arching, and to determine the various degrees of thickness in a more rigorous manner. His varnish became more highly coloured, and, in a word, his productions assumed a different aspect; but we still discern in them some traditions of the school of Nicholas Amati. Violin makers of the present day habitually designate them by the name of *Stradivarius-Amatis*.

In 1700 the artist had attained to his fifty-sixth year; his talent was then in its full vigour, and from that period to 1725 the instruments which came from his hands are perfect masterpieces. He no longer felt his way; but, being certain of all that he did, he carried his manufacture, even to the minutest details, to the highest possible finish. His model has all the amplitude desirable; the outlines of it are designed with a taste and a purity which, after a century and a half, still excite the admiration of connoiseurs. The wood, selected with the keenest discernment, unites to richness of figure all the conditions of sonority. For the back, as well as for the sides, he then altered the disposition of it, having the timber cut on the quarter (*sur maille*) instead of on the layers (*sur couche*). The arching of his instruments, without being too elevated, falls off in gentle and regular curves, which leaves it all the requisite flexibility. The sound-holes, cut with the hand of a master, became models for shape and size (*modèles de dispositions*) to all his successors. The scroll, which had assumed a more severe character, is carved with great perfection. The beautiful, warm tone of the varnish of Stradivarius takes its date from this period: the quality of it is fine and extremely supple.

The workmanship of the interior of the instrument displays no less perfection; all is there finished with the greatest care. The degrees of thickness are adjusted in a rational manner, and are remarkable for a precision which could not have been attained except by long study. The back, the belly, and all the parts of which the instrument is composed, are in a perfectly harmonious relation. It was, doubtless, repeated trials and diligent observations which also led Stradivarius, throughout this period of his productive career, to make the blocks and the sides of his violins of sallow, the specific lightness of which surpasses that of every other wood. In short, every thing has been foreseen, calculated and determined with certainty, in these admirable instruments. The bar alone is too weak, in consequence of the gradual rise in the pitch, from the beginning of the eighteenth century; the inevitable result of which has been a considerable increase of tension and a much greater pressure exercised on the belly. Hence the necessity has arisen for re-barring all the old violins and violoncellos.

At the same period when Stradivarius had acquired the perfection which is here related, and when he worked with certainty as to the results, he has sometimes departed from his established type, in order to satisfy the fancies of artists or amateurs. Thus it happens that he has made violins of a more elongated pattern, whose appearance has less grace, although the same care has presided over their manufacture: indeed, every part of them is proportioned to this modification of their form, in order to maintain the equilibrium in the vibrations. In these, as in the other instruments which left the artist's hands at this period of his life, the tone possesses that noble energy, that brilliance and distinctive character which have every where established the great renown of Stradivarius.

The instruments produced by Stradivarius from 1725 to 1730 are also very good; though the workmanship no longer displays the same perfection. The swell or arching is somewhat more rounded, which slightly impairs the clearness of the sound; the delicacy and finish of the work progressively decrease, and the varnish is brown. There seems also to have been a falling off in the manufacture; for we meet with proportionably fewer instruments of this period than of the preceding.

In 1730, and even somewhat earlier, the impress of the master almost entirely disappeared. A practised eye discovers that the instruments have been made by less able hands. He himself signed many of them as having been made simply under his direction: "*sub disciplina Stradivarii.*" In others we recognize the hand of Charles Bergonzi, and of the sons of Stradivarius, *Omobono* and *Francesco*. After the death of this celebrated man, many instruments which remained unfinished in his workshop were completed by his sons. The greater number bear his name on the printed label, and hence arises the uncertainty and confusion in regard to the products of the latter times.

Stradivarius made but few altos, all of which are of a large size. Their quality of tone is extremely beautiful, being penetrating, noble, and sympathetic.

The violoncellos of his make are more numerous: in them we notice the same progressive steps towards perfection of workmanship and admirable finish, as in the violins. These instruments are of two dimensions: the one large, to which the name of *bass* was formerly given; the other smaller, which is the *violoncello* proper. To the first of these categories belongs the bass of M. Servais, Professor at the Royal Conservatory of Brussels, and a *virtuoso* whose renown is European. The tone of this fine instrument has an extraordinary power, united to silvery mellowness. The violoncello of the admirable artist M. Franchomme is of the other pattern; it formerly belonged to Duport, and is an instrument of very great value. At the present day this pattern is preferred, the dimensions of which are convenient for the performance of difficulties. The hand of a Servais is required for a bass so large as his.

The violoncellos of Stradivarius are immeasurably superior to all other instruments of this kind: their powerful tone possesses a fulness, a distinctive character and a brilliance which cannot be equalled. These admirable qualities result, on the one hand, from the choice of the wood, on the other, from the degrees of thickness; and, in short, from the exact relations of all parts of the instrument, which are set in equilibrium in order that the vibrations may be free, energetic, and prolonged. The superiority of these instruments is ensured, as in the case of the violins, by the constant application of the laws of acoustics.

At the period when Stradivarius worked, viols of all species were still used in the orchestras; he himself made many of them, of different forms and dimensions, with six and seven strings, as well as quintons with flat backs, raised sides, and arched bellies; also some guitars, lutes, and mandoras. One of the latter instruments, constructed by this great artist, exists at Paris, at the present time: the delicacy of the workmanship and the beauty of the varnish are very remarkable; the carving of the head is of exquisite finish, so that, both as a whole, as well as in its details, this pretty instrument combines all kinds of perfection.

Two things are equally worthy of attention in the labours of Anthony Stradivarius; namely, the excellence and the almost infinite number of his instruments. It is true that the multiplicity of his productions is explained by the great age to which he arrived, and by his perseverance in working, which he maintained to the end of his life. Stradivarius was one of those few men who, in aiming at perfection, so far as it is possible for humanity to attain to it, never swerve from the path which may conduct them thereto: men who suffer nothing to divert or turn them aside from their object; who are not discouraged by fallacies, but who, full of faith in the value of the object they have in view, as well as in their ability for its realisation, continually recommence that which they have done well, in order to arrive at the best possible result. To Stradivarius, the making of stringed instruments was the whole world; thereon he concentrated his entire self. In this way only can a man raise himself, when aptitude answers to the will. The prolonged existence of ninety-three years, which was that of the artist who is the subject of this notice, was entirely passed away in a quiet workshop, before a bench, with compass or tool in hand.

We have before seen that Anthony Stradivari finished a violin at the age of ninety-two years, in 1736. For some years previously, he had been preparing himself for death, having made ready his tomb in 1729. The proof of this is to be seen in the following extract from the book of inscriptions of Cremona (*Inscriptiones Cremonenses universæ*), which has been already mentioned. The extract runs in these terms:

"Finalmente nello stesso volume a pag. CXXXII, No. 923,
"leggesi la Epigrafe del sepolcro del celebre fabbricatore di
"violini Antonio Stradivari, che era già nel Pavimento, intera-
"mente rifatto della Chiesa di San Domenico de Padri
": Domenicani ed è la seguente:

Sepolcro. Di
Antonio. Stradivari
E. suoi. Eredi. An. 1729.

" In fede di quanto sopra,
" Cremona, le 18 Settembre, 1855.
" Il Prelato Primicerio Antonio Dragoni,
" Ex Vicario Generale Capitolare
" della Città e diocesi di Cremona."*

Then follow three seals displaying the arms, names, and titles of the chief prelate Anthony Dragoni.

The date, 1729, placed on the tomb of Stradivari, led to the belief that he had died at that period; but the discovery of a violin of 1736, in which Stradivari himself had stated his age to be ninety-two years, has completely subverted that tradition. Some new researches, made with indefatigable perseverance, have

---

* " Finally, in the same volume, at page CXXXII, No. 923, we read
" the epitaph of the tomb of the celebrated violin-maker, Anthony
" Stradivari, which was formerly in the pavement—[now] entirely
" relaid—of St. Dominic's Church, of the Dominican Fathers, and is
" as follows:

Sepulchre. Of
Anthony. Stradivari
And. his. Heirs. Year 1729.

" In testimony of the above,
" Cremona, the 18th of September 1855.
" Anthony Dragoni, Chief Prelate (or Dean),
" Capitular Ex-vicar general
" of the city and diocese of Cremona."

been finally crowned with success, and have made known the precise date of the decease of this celebrated artist. In an authentic extract from the registers of the Cathedral of Cremona, signed and delivered by M. Julius Fusetti, vicar of that church, we have the proof that Anthony Stradivari was buried on the 19th of December, 1737, and consequently that he died on the 17th or 18th of the same month, at the full age of ninety-three years. But, by an inexplicable singularity, neither his own remains, nor those of his children, were deposited in the tomb which he had prepared for them; for the burial extract is worded as follows:

"Nel libro col titolo: *Libro de' Morti* nella Chiesa di
" S. Domenico, essistante nell' archivio di questa parocchia
" trovasi quanto segue:

"A dì 19 Dicembre 1737. Dato sepoltura al fù sig.
" Antonio Stradivari, sepolto nella sepoltura del sig. Francesco
" Vilani, nella Capella del Rosario, parocchia di S. Mateo.

" Dalla Cattedrale di Cremona,
" Li 19 Settembre, 1855.

In fede

Signé: *Fusetti Giulio Vic°*.*

(with the church seal).

---

* "In the book entitled: *Libro de' morti (Burial Register)* of the
" Church of St. Dominic, existing in the archives of this parish, we
" find the following:

"On the 19th day of December, 1737: Took place the funeral of
" the late Signor Antonio Stradivari, who was buried in the vault of
" Signor Francesco Vilani, in the chapel of the Rosary, in the parish
" of St. Matthew.

" From the Cathedral of Cremona,
" The 19th of September, 1855.

In testimony

Signed: *Julius Fusetti, Vicar.*"

Anthony Stradivarius had been married and had had three sons and one daughter. The sons were named *Francesco, Omobono*, and the third *Paolo*. The first two worked in their father's shop until his death; but Paolo entered into [other] business. If Catharine, the daughter of Stradivarius, was his first child, we might pretty nearly determine the period of his marriage; for she died in 1748, at about the age of seventy years, according to an extract from the burial register of the Cathedral of Cremona, from 1730 to 1752.* It follows, from this date, and from the age at which she had arrived, that she was born about the year 1678; from whence we may conclude that the marriage of Anthony Stradivarius must have taken place in 1676 or 1677, that is, when he was twenty-two or twenty-three years of age.

The life of Anthony Stradivarius was as tranquil as his calling was peaceful. The year 1702, alone, must have caused him much disquiet, when, during the war concerning the Succession, the city of Cremona was taken by Marshal Villeroy on the Imperial side, retaken by Prince Eugène, and finally taken a third time by the French: but, after that period, Italy enjoyed a long tranquillity, in which the old age of the artist glided peacefully away. We know but little respecting that

---

* "Catarina, figlia del fù Antonio Stradivari, domiciliata sotto la "parocchia della catedrale di Cremona, more nell' anno 1748, nell' età "di circa 70, e fù sepolta nella chiesa di S. Domenico. *Libro de' morti* "*del* 1730 *al* 1752.

" (Catharine, daughter of the late Antonio Stradivari, dwelling in "the parish of the Cathedral of Cremona, died in the year 1748, at "about the age of 70 years, and was buried in the church of St. "Dominic. *Burial Register from* 1730 *to* 1752.)"

uneventful existence. Polledro, late first violin at the Chapel Royal of Turin, who died a few years ago, at a very advanced age, declared that his master had known Stradivarius, and that he was fond of talking about him. He was, he said, tall and thin. Habitually covered with a cap of white wool in winter, and of cotton in summer, he wore over his clothes an apron of white leather when he worked; and, as he was always working, his costume scarcely ever varied. He had acquired more than competency by labour and economy; for the inhabitants of Cremona were accustomed to say: "*rich as Stradivari.*" Old La Houssaie, whom I knew in my youth, and who had visited Cremona a short time after the death of Stradivarius, told me that the price which he asked for his violins was *four louis d'or* [£4]. At this rate, and considering the period when he lived, he must certainly have acquired some wealth. Bergonzi, grandson of Charles (the best pupil of Stradivarius, except Guarnerius), who died a few years ago at the age of eighty, pointed out the place where the celebrated artist worked, in a house numbered 1239, in St. Dominic's Square, opposite the *Porta Maggiore*. Since then, this shop was long occupied by a cooper; but it is now in the occupation of an upholsterer. These details may possess some interest for the ardent admirers of the beautiful instruments of Stradivarius.

The question has been often raised, whether Stradivarius was guided, in the making of his instruments, by any other principles than those of a long acquaintance with facts; and whether the excellence of these instruments is not simply the result of such experience, and especially of the effect of time upon the wood of which they are formed? To say the truth, this question is generally answered mentally before putting it; for I scarcely know a violin-maker who is not persuaded that no instrument can become good until it has been much played upon, and until time has deprived the wood of which it is made of all those properties which are injurious to a fine quality of tone. Now, since this is a question of facts, there are some absolutely opposed to these prejudices: the first of which is, that there exists at this moment, in Paris, a Stradivarius violin, made in 1716, which, after having reposed during sixty years in the collection of Count Cozio de Salabue, was purchased by Louis Tarisio, in 1824, and has since become the property of M. Vuillaume: but this instrument has never been played upon.* The wood of which it is made is of the choicest description, and remarkable for the richness of its waves. The workmanship is perfection, and the varnish beautiful: in short, nothing is wanting in it. It is a new violin, apparently just out of the maker's hand; and is, finally, the sole instrument of Stradivarius which has come down to us in this state of preservation. Now, this genuine memorial of ancient manufacture—this instrument which has not resounded under the action of the bow during the space of nearly a century and a half which has elapsed since the period of its fabrication—this instrument gives a striking refutation to the idea, that a free and pure tone cannot be

---

* The reader will at once perceive, from the context, that these words are not to be taken in an absolute sense.—TR.

produced from a violin or a bass until after it has been long in use; for here, in this new instrument, we find all the qualities combined of *power, mellowness, roundness, delicacy, free vibration, a very superior, noble and penetrating tone.* In a word, this violin is a type of external beauty, and of sonorous perfection.

In regard to the beneficial effects produced on instruments by time—by which, according to the vulgar opinion, the violins of Stradivarius and Guarnerius have attained a portion of their finest qualities—it seems to be forgotten that those of Bocquay, Pierret, Despont, Véron, Guersan, Castagnéry, Saint-Paul, and Salomon, are at least as old as those of Stradivarius, and yet at the present day a *hundred francs* [£4] could not be obtained even for the best of them. It is likewise forgotten that the Tyrolese makers, who lived in the seventeenth and the early part of the eighteenth century, have also had the benefit of time for their instruments, and that they had the opportunity of selecting equally good wood; but who would pretend to institute a comparison between their productions and those of the two great masters above-mentioned?

Something more than time, then, is required, to impart a fine quality of tone to instruments; and even something more than a form of construction agreeable to the eye: regard must be had to the laws of acoustics, and these are what have to be discovered.

The laws of acoustics, like all those of physical science—that is, of nature—are laws of relation. Every phenomenon, in fact, results from relations between certain elements and certain others. Had Stradivarius discovered these laws? Unquestionably, no: but, like a superior man in his art, he had made practical experiments; and what his researches and experience thus enabled him to do with certainty, is precisely the result of acoustical laws, as since formulated by a learned philosopher from the productions of the artist himself. Take him at his starting point, and what do we find in the instruments of his master? A tone, pure, silvery and mellow; workmanship of careful finish; but an absence of intensity in the sound of the instrument, resulting from too elevated an arching, and a defect in certain proportions. Stradivarius himself remained subject to the like conditions for some years, and only abandoned them by degrees. What induced him thus to modify his instruments so very progressively? Evidently, the desire to impart to them qualities which were wanting in those of his predecessors. Foreseeing, then, the possibility of these qualities, he very naturally sought to attain them.

In 1700, his ideas became settled; his model was decided on, and his hand, skilful to second his intelligent views, gave to the form of his instruments all the perfection desirable. That which was wanting to the Amati—power united with brilliancy and mellowness— he had discovered. He did what he wished, because he knew what was required. Was this effected by chance? No; as we shall proceed to prove.

A man endowed with the rarest powers for the observation of facts and for the deductions which might be drawn from them, Felix Savart, too early lost to science, was, for nearly twenty years, absorbed in the problem of the laws by which the best possible tone might be produced in bow-instruments; and having duly considered all the various theories on this subject, he finally resolved to submit the instruments of Stradivarius to analysis, hoping to derive therefrom the illumination which he had been unable to obtain elsewhere. As he himself declared, in his course of lectures on experimental philosophy, delivered in the college of France during the academic year 1838—9, he was indebted to the courtesy of M. Vuillaume, and to his zeal for science, for the opportunity of experimenting upon a great number of violins by Stradivarius and Guarnerius, as well as on the remains of instruments by these great masters. It was from the result of these reiterated experiments, varied in a thousand ways, that the learned Professor deduced his theory of the construction of bow-instruments, the principles of which he detailed in his course, and of which he was preparing a definite abstract, which death unfortunately prevented him from finishing and publishing. It is from these researches that I borrow what follows.

It is at once evident that all the doubts which perplexed the mind of Savart, concerning the laws that govern the construction of bow-instruments, were immediately dispelled when he experimented on the instruments of the grand epoch of Stradivarius; because there he always found the same results produced by the same causes, the same forms, and the same proportions. Sagacious as any one could be, in the art of discovering these causes, by experiments as well conceived as they were nicely carried out, Savart was able, at the close of them, to determine the laws which (even without his knowing it) had directed our celebrated artist in his labours.

In general terms, the instruments of Stradivarius owe their admirable qualities: first, to the excellent choice of the wood; secondly, to the relations of sonority subsisting among the different pieces which compose these instruments; thirdly, to the capaciousness of the chest, combined with the proportions of thickness of the back and belly, from whence results the sound produced by the vibrations of the air under the action of the bow, which sets the sonorous body in motion; lastly, to the very exact precision of the workmanship, and to the varnish, whose essential properties are to protect the wood against the influence of the hygrometric changes of the atmosphere, without offering any obstacle to the elasticity on which the freedom of vibration depends.

In analysing the instruments of Stradivarius, it was requisite to begin with an analysis of the sonority of the wood used by him. The appearance of it is of no assistance whatever as a guide to facts, in this respect; the most practised eye can discern nothing therein: carefully conducted experiments can alone afford any information.

That all kinds of wood yield a sound, no one can doubt: but by what method can they be examined in order to determine their intonation? The specific sonority of wood was already known at the period when Mersenne published his *Traité de l'Harmonie universelle* (1636); he speaks of it, and indicates percussion as the means for knowing and determining it. No doubt this method was adopted by Stradivarius; indeed, we shall find a proof of it in what follows. But, in the first place, let it be observed that the experiments and discoveries of Chladni, on the vibrations of sonorous plates of all kinds, have made known a preferable method to percussion for determining the specific intonations of woods of given dimensions: this method consists in the friction of a bow against the edges of a rod suitably prepared. But such a dimension of rod had to be sought, from which might be obtained with facility a sound sufficiently intense to be accurately appreciated, in order that the intonation might be determined and compared with other sounds produced likewise by the friction of the bow.

Some fragments of instruments by Stradivarius presented dimensions large enough to admit of rectangular rods being made out of them—cut perpendicularly, and parallel to the fibres of the wood—of a length of 20 centimètres [7.874 in.], a breadth of 20 millimètres [.787 in.], and a thickness of 5 millimètres [.197 in.]. These rods were alternately put into vibration, by holding the one under examination between the fingers, in such a way as to touch it only at points a quarter of the length from each end, and presenting the side of the thickness to the action of the bow, precisely at the middle of the length. On the upper surface of the rod, some fine, dry sand was scattered, and, in order to leave this surface perfectly free, the rod was held at one end, between the first finger and thumb, and sustained horizontally with the little finger underneath. In this position, and with the bow in action, the sand was seen to divide itself into two parallel lines on the sides of the rod; thus proving that the whole rod had entered into regular vibrations.

These experiments yielded the following results:—

1. A rod of well-figured maple, of the dimensions stated, obtained from a fragment of a violin of Stradivarius, made in 1717, produced the note A sharp:

2. Another rod of plain maple, a fragment of an instrument of the same master, made in 1708, gave the same note.

3. A rod of deal taken from a violin of Stradivarius, made in 1724, produced F:

4. Another rod of deal, from an instrument of the same master, made in 1690, gave the same note.

5. Lastly, a third rod of deal obtained from another instrument of this celebrated maker, bearing the date 1730, also gave the same note.

The pitch having continually risen during the last quarter of a century, the ancient standard was used, in making these experiments, which gave for the [lowest] C of the violin 512 vibrations in a second.

Results so identical, produced by wood employed at such distant periods, leave no doubt that Stradivarius made use of means analogous to those adopted by Savart in his experiments, and that he attached great importance to them: for his eye-sight, however keen and well-practised it might have been, could never have enabled him to judge beforehand of the intonation of the wood which he used. This is proved by the fact that experiments of the same kind, made on various woods whose appearance was identical, and with rods of the same dimensions, have yielded extreme diversities of sound, such as a third, a fourth, and even more, when the rods were not taken from the same piece of wood.

Let us now see what of positive instruction theory has deduced from the facts which have been mentioned, and why we may conclude with certainty that the admirable qualities of the instruments of Stradivarius have been obtained by virtue of the laws of this theory, and not by the effect of time and use, which can never bring forth perfection from a mediocre article.

We know that the sound-board or belly, which supports the strings and the bridge, is made of deal, and the back of the instrument, of maple. Deal is preferable to every other kind of wood for the belly, by reason of its feeble density, and especially on account of its elasticity.* Its resistance to flexion is greater, not only than that of any other wood, but even than that of many metallic bodies. It is equal to that of glass, and even steel, over which it has the advantage of exceeding lightness. Sound is propagated with as great a rapidity in deal, as in the other substances which have been mentioned. This fact is demonstrated by the following experiment: if we take three rods of glass, steel, and deal cut in the direction of the fibres, all having the

---

* We here reproduce a part of what we have said in our *Rapport sur les instruments de musique de l' Exposition de* 1855, concerning the theory of bow-instruments.

same dimensions, and if we cause them to vibrate longitudinally or transversely, so as to make them produce the same kind of vibratory division, the intonation of the sound rendered by the three rods will be precisely the same; which would not be the case with a rod of any other wood than deal. Thus, the rapidity of sound is as great in deal, as in glass or steel, where it is great in an eminent degree; and, besides, deal offers the important advantage of presenting a large resisting surface to the flexion [inevitable] in a thin belly like that of a violin, and of possessing the greatest elasticity possible.

Maple is preferable to every other kind of wood, for the back of bow-instruments : the great masters of the ancient school of Italy never used any other. In maple, the propagation of sound is much less rapid than in deal; in the latter, it is from fifteen to sixteen and a half times quicker than in the air; while, in maple, it is only from ten to twelve times quicker than in the aerial waves. Hence it follows, that if we make two rods of precisely the same dimensions, one of deal and the other of maple, the sound of the deal rod will be perceptibly higher than that of the maple. Consequently, the belly and the back of a violin, being of the same size, do not possess an identical intonation. We shall see, presently, the importance of these data.

Let us now examine in what relation the back and belly should stand [to each other] before they are united. This it was not possible to determine, until after re-repeated and carefully-conducted experiments. A violin was constructed with a back and belly of deal, perfectly in unison, and the tone proved to be weak and dull;

a maple back was then substituted for the deal one, also in unison, but the instrument was utterly bad and the quality of tone very weak. The cause of this phenomenon was easily discovered; for, maple not being endowed with the like degree of rapidity in the propagation of sound-waves as deal, it is evident that the back of the instrument could not be put in unison with the belly, except by making it too thick. Hence, these facts clearly prove that the back and belly ought not to be in unison. Not only should they not be so, but they should be decidedly kept distant from it; in order to avoid the beatings always consequent on two sounds which approximate in their intonation. To determine the relation of the sounds which the back and belly should yield, so as to obtain the best resonance possible, it was necessary to resort to direct experiments, which were made conjointly by Savart and M. Vuillaume on several very valuable instruments of Stradivarius and Guarnerius. The [true] sounds of the back and belly were ascertained in the following manner: these pieces were fastened in a wooden vice, at a point where two nodal lines crossed each other, the one transversal and the other longitudinal, answering to the two kinds of elasticity of deal and maple. When they were put into vibration by the bow, longitudinal and transversal lines were produced,* which proved that the two kinds of elasticity were in action, and the nodal system being the same both on the back and on the belly, it was found there was *a tone*

---

* The wooden plates forming the back and belly were previously sprinkled with dry, fine sand.—TR.

difference between them. The back was exactly one tone lower than the belly.

For contradictory experiments, a back and belly were constructed in other relations: when nearly in unison, beatings resulted; and when farther apart than an interval of a tone, they no longer vibrated conjointly in a normal manner.

Here, then, is a new fact acquired for science: the maple plate, or the back of the violin, should be a tone lower than the deal plate [or belly], in order to obtain the finest sonority possible when they are united. Can it be supposed to be by mere chance that this relation is invariably found in the excellent instruments of Stradivarius and Guarnerius, and that the first of these masters, of whom the other was the pupil, had no method for determining the said relation, of which his great experience and practical skill had incontestably recognised the necessity? Chance may give rise to a fact in one instance, but it never regularly repeats the same.

We now come to another point no less essential. The intensity of the sounds rendered by a violin depends on the mass of air contained within it, which ought to be in a certain relation with the other elements; a relation which it is here the question to determine. By a series of ingenious experiments, made with an apparatus which permitted the mass of air contained in a violin to be augmented or diminished [at pleasure], we are assured that, if the strings are put into vibration while the mass of air is at a medium, we obtain sounds at once mellow and powerful; if the volume of air be too great, the grave sounds are weak and dull, and the acute harsh and thin; if it be too little, the grave sounds are coarse, and those of the first string lose their brilliance.

If we examine the sound produced by the air in the chest when the tone rendered by the strings is most beautiful and intense, we find that it keeps within certain limits which depend on the form and the other elements of the instrument. In trying the mass of air contained in several [instruments of] Stradivarius, by means of a wind-conductor formed of a simple brass tube, slightly conical, and flat at its larger end, so as to leave only a little slit for the escape of the air, it was found, by placing the flat end of this apparatus over one of the f holes and blowing through the other end, that the air always produced a sound corresponding to 512 vibrations in a second, which was that of [middle] C, in the time of Stradivarius; but which, in 1838, when Savart made his experiments, answered to B natural [a semitone below]. Through the excessive rise in the pitch for about the last eighteen years, the sound produced by 512 vibrations is now nearly in unison with B flat. All the excellent violins of Stradivarius and Guarnerius have yielded the same result. This, then, is another fact acquired for science: the air contained in a violin should produce a sound equal to 512 vibrations in a second, when set in motion by the apparatus of which we have spoken. If the intonation of the air be higher, the grave sounds of the instrument are dry; if lower, the sounds of the first string are of difficult emission, and those of the fourth resemble those of the alto.

It will perhaps be asked whether Stradivarius made all these experiments. Doubtless, he did not; but it is certain that, since he always arrived at the same results in regard to the quantity of air contained in the body of his instruments, he had observed, from an attentive study of his own productions, that the capacity, both by the curve of the arching and by the height of the sides in relation with the pattern of the violin, should be in certain proportions which he was always able to realize by the marvellous dexterity of his hand. Here, again, be it observed, chance does not uniformly repeat the same effects.

The f holes in the belly exercise an important influence on the mass of air contained in the instrument. It has been noticed that, when a strip of paper is glued over one of them, the sound of the mass is perceptibly lowered, and the tone of the instrument becomes changed in a remarkable manner. The consequence of this experiment is that, if the holes are too small, the sound of the air will be too low, and the signal defects above-mentioned will declare themselves. If, on the contrary, the holes are too large, the sound of the air will be too high. Such is actually the case in a violin of large pattern by Maggini, the mass of air in which ought to yield a lower sound than that of 512 vibrations in a second, but which, on the contrary, produces a higher sound, because the f holes are larger than those of Stradivarius; this circumstance, however, is an exception in the instruments of that master. It is by such observations as these that we have obtained proof of the care which this great artist took to establish a perfect harmony in all the parts of his instruments, so that they might be always in a state of equilibrium. We know what absolute regularity he has always displayed in the cutting of the f holes, invariably so true and graceful!

Sometimes this great master departed from his accustomed dimensions, either for the sake of experiment, or to gratify the taste of artists and amateurs who desired of him a certain special quality of tone; but precisely in such instances is found the most striking demonstration of the excellence of the principles which guided him in the construction of so large a number of his perfect instruments. There are some violins of Stradivarius perceptibly larger than his ordinary pattern, and in which the mass of air is not in exact relation with the resonance of the back and belly; as a consequence, these instruments are inferior to the others. The reason of the excellence of the violins, altos, and basses of Stradivarius—or, to speak more correctly, of all instruments of this species—lies in the perfect equilibrium of all the parts. So, be it observed, that two violins, one of Stradivarius and the other of Guarnerius, having considerable analogy in their forms and dimensions, and both possessing the like harmonious proportions, have a remarkable resemblance in their tone, and equally rank among the best instruments which have emanated from these great masters.

The necessity of harmony in the proportions is observable throughout. If the back or the belly be too thin, the tone of the instrument will be feeble; if too thick, the emission of the sounds will be laborious and obstinate: the excess of thickness will nullify the advantages which the wood should present by its rapid transmission of sonorous waves and its very acute specific sonority. If too great a bulge be given to the belly, or the arching be too elevated, the equilibrium of the mass of air will be destroyed, and the tone of the instrument will become dull and nasal.

The height of the sides is likewise of the greatest importance; for it is that which determines the capacity of the chest in its relations with the model of the back and belly, and which, consequently, decides the quantity of air introduced in the instrument. And it is here that the action of the mass of air contained in a sonorous chest displays its importance in regard to the production of the sounds. In giving to a violoncello proportional dimensions to those of a violin, and in the relations previously indicated, the back and belly should be 35 inches [long], by 20 inches wide; because the A of this instrument is a twelfth below the first string of the violin, and it is requisite that the volume of sound should be proportioned to the gravity of the intonation; but these great dimensions would be inconvenient for playing. Stradivarius gave to the back and belly of his violoncellos a length of only 26 or 27 inches, and a width of 15 or 16, at the most; but he provided, in the height of the sides, a compensation necessary for the mass of air, in making them 4 inches instead of three, which would have been the exact proportion if the back and belly had been larger. It is compulsory to adopt the proportions of Stradivarius and Guarnerius for the height of the sides of violins, in order to put the sound of the mass of air in harmonic relation with that of the back and belly.

The bar glued under the belly of the violin, on the left of the bridge, is now too weak in the old instruments, particularly in those of Stradivarius and Guarnerius: in all of them it has been found necessary to replace it by a stronger one. But we must not conclude that these masters were mistaken in this part of their work: they proportioned the bar to the pressure of the strings on the belly, conformably to the pitch of their day. Tartini found, by experiments made in 1734, that the pressure of the four strings on the instrument was equal to 63 pounds. It must be observed that the strings of Tartini were smaller than those with which violins are now mounted, and that his bridge was lower, so that the angle formed by the strings was considerably less. Twenty years ago,* the first string required a weight of 22 pounds in order to bring it up to pitch, and the other strings a little less; so that the total pressure was, then, about 80 pounds. After 1734, the pitch was raised a semitone, the instruments were mounted with thicker strings, and the angle which they formed on the bridge was more acute: hence the necessity of re-barring the violins. Since then, so excessive has been the rise in pitch, through the craving for a brilliant sonority, that there is nearly a difference of a semitone between the pitch of 1830 and that of 1856.

---

* This was written by M. Fétis in 1855.—Tr.

If a new experiment were now made to ascertain the pressure of the four strings on the belly of a violin, no doubt it would be found greatly augmented. This enormous weight incessantly tends to effect the destruction of the old instruments, and demands increased power of resistance in the bar underneath the bridge. Such is the real cause of the necessity of substituting for the old, weak bar, in the violins of Stradivarius, one of stronger proportions.

Most of the violin makers are ignorant that it is with this appendage, as with the back and belly of the instrument. The wood whose sonority, in given dimensions, is the most acute under the action of the bow, is that which should be preferred for the construction of the bar; because, as before stated, in these conditions the vibrations are more prompt and free. The same is true, in regard to the wood of which the bridge is made.

If it were necessary to prove, otherwise than by results, the profound knowledge which the celebrated makers of Cremona possessed of all the phenomena of resonance in their instruments, it would suffice to examine the form of the bridge, and to follow the experiments of Savart on this essential part of the sounding apparatus. How many conjectures must they not have made before arriving at the knowledge of the necessity of all the incisions seen in the present bridge, which even artists themselves merely view as ornaments! From the immense number of differently shaped bridges which have come down to us, I have chosen only two varieties of viol bridges, one belonging to a viol with seven strings, the body of which is not cut out, except at the two sides (*Fig.* 1), and the other

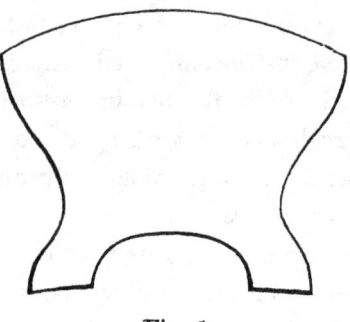

Fig. 1.

obtained from a viol with five strings, cut through in every part (*Fig.* 2); next, two violin bridges, the first

Fig. 2.

from a small-pattern violin of the ancient school of

Anthony Amati (*Fig.* 3), the other having been used

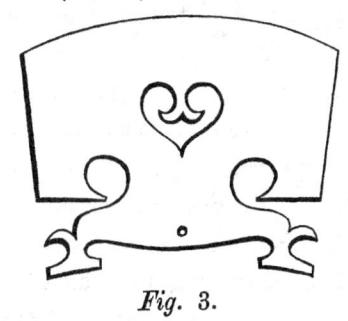

Fig. 3.

in fitting up a Nicholas Amati (*Fig.* 4). The two latter

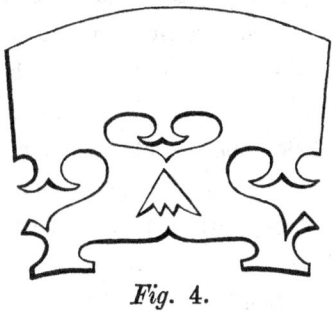

Fig. 4.

already belong to the definitive form of the bridge, but with certain variations, either in the number of the incisions, or in their shape. It was Stradivarius who definitively established the existing form, represented below (*Fig.* 5). Delicate experiments, made with the

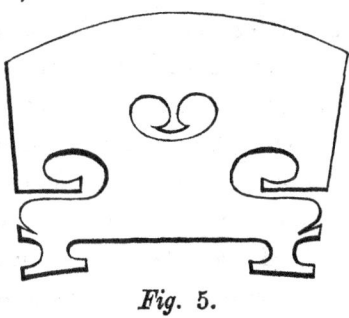

Fig. 5.

minutest care, have demonstrated that any modifications introduced into this model tend to impair the sonority of a good instrument.

Thus, it appears that the beautiful experiments of Savart have proved, to a demonstration, the excellence of the principles which guided Stradivarius in the making of the fine instruments produced by him from 1700 to 1725. Nor did he swerve from them in his later works; but the great age to which he had attained gradually diminished his firmness of hand. The form is not essentially changed in his latest instruments, but the workmanship betrays timidity. His finest instruments known are: 1st. That which belongs to the Grand Duke of Tuscany; 2nd. M. Alard's; 3rd. Viotti's, now belonging to M. Brochant de Villiers; 4th. Artot's, which is in the possession of the Count de Cessol, at Nice; 5th. M. Boissier's, of Geneva; and, lastly, those of Messrs. Betts, Goding, Plowdens, and Fountain, of London.

These principles, so rich in results, the master communicated to his best immediate pupils, at the head of whom stand Joseph Guarnerius, an original but capricious genius; next, Charles Bergonzi, the most exact imitator of his master, and of whose make there are some excellent instruments. Francis Stradivarius has likewise made some good violins, which, from 1725 to about 1740, bear his name; but we know others made by him in conjunction with his brother, Omobono, which bear this inscription: *Sotto la disciplina d'A. Stradivarius, Cremona.* Omobono Stradivarius was more particularly occupied with the repair and fitting-up of instruments, than with their manufacture. He died early in June, 1742, and was interred on the 9th of that month, as is proved by an authentic extract [from the register] of the Church of St. Dominic, at Cremona.* His brother, Francis, survived him only eleven months, having been buried the 13th of May, 1743, as shown by an extract from the same register.† Both brothers were laid in the same tomb with their father.

The other immediate pupils of Anthony Stradivarius are Michael Angelo Bergonzi, of Cremona; Laurence Guadagnini, also of Cremona; Francis Gobetti, of Venice, and Alexander Galiano, of Naples. They are here arranged in chronological order according to their productions:

1st. Franciscus Gobettus, Venetiis.......... 1690 to 1720
2nd. Alexander Galianus, Neapoli.......... 1695 to 1725
3rd. Lorenzo Guadagnini, Cremonæ.......... 1695 to 1740
4th. Homobonus Stradivarius { sub disciplina } 1700 to 1725
5th. Franciscus Stradivarius { A. Stradivarii }
6th. Homobonus Stradivarius, Cremonæ...... 1725 to 1740
7th. Franciscus Stradivarius, Cremonæ...... 1725 to 1730
8th. Carlo Bergonzi, Cremonæ.............. 1720 to 1750
9th. Michael Angelo Bergonzi, Cremonæ...... 1725 to 1750

---

* A dì 9 Giugno 1742.—Dato sepoltura al fù sig[r]. Omobono Stradivari, sepolto nella capella del Rosario, nella sepoltura del sig[r]. Francesco Vilani, Parocchia di S. Mateo.—In fede, Fusetti Giulio vic[o].

(On the 9th day of June, 1742.—Took place the funeral of the late Sig[r]. Omobono Stradivari, who was buried in the chapel of the Rosary, in the vault of Sig[r]. Francesco Vilani, in the Parish of St. Matthew. —In testimony, Julius Fusetti, Vicar).

† A dì 13 Maggio, 1743.—Dato sepoltura al fù sig[r]. Francesco Stradivari, sepolto nella capella del Rosario, nella sepoltura del sig[r]. Francesco Vilani, Parocchia di S. Mateo.—In fede, Fusetti Giulio vic[o].

(On the 13th day of May, 1743.—Took place the funeral of the late Sig[r]. Francesco Stradivari, who was buried in the chapel of the Rosary, in the vault of Sig[r]. Francesco Vilani, in the Parish of St. Matthew.— In testimony, Julius Fusetti, Vicar).

Among the Italian violin makers of the third class, some were pupils of the Amati school; others were formed by the immediate pupils of Anthony Stradivarius. These may be placed in the following chronological order:

Pietro della Costa, of Trevisa................	1660 to 1680
Michael Angelo Garani, of Bologna..........	1685 to 1715
David Teckler, of Rome....................	1690 to 1735
Carlo Guiseppe Testore, of Milan............	1690 to 1700
Carlo Antonio Testore, of Milan............	1700 to 1730
Paolo Antonio Testore, of Milan............	1710 to 1745
Nicolo Galiano, of Naples..................	1700 to 1740
Gennaro Galiano, of Naples................	1710 to 1750
Spiritus Sursano, of Coni (Cunco)..........	1714 to 1720
Tomaso Balestiere, of Mantua..............	1720 to 1750
Ferdinando Galiano, son of Nicolo, of Naples..	1740 to 1780
Giovanni Battista Guadagnini, of Piacenza....	1755 to 1785
Carlo Landolfi, of Milan...................	1750 to 1760
Alessandro Zanti, of Mantua...............	1770
Laurentius Sturionus (Storioni), of Cremona..	1780 to 1795

Some makers, born in foreign countries, were formed in Italy in the school of the Amati, or in that of Anthony Stradivari. At their head stands James Stainer,[*] originally from the Tyrol, and founder of a school of violin makers in that country. He was

---

[*] This maker is better known in England as *Jacob* Stainer (or Steiner), but the Latin labels on his instruments reading "*Jacobus Stainer in Absom &c.*" justify M. Fétis, both here and in his "*Biographie des Musiciens*," in calling him *James* (*Jacques*). For additional remarks on his violins, see the translator's edition of Otto's "*Treatise on the Structure and Preservation of the Violin*," published by Messrs. Cocks & Co.—Tr.

born at Absom, near Hall, about three quarters of a league from Inspruck, and in his youth worked at Cremona, with Nicholas Amati. The history of this artist is enveloped in obscurity and has the appearance of romance; but it may be confidently asserted that he was a great master. His glory was obscured, and his instruments have not the commercial value which belongs to such as really came from his hands; for the Tyrolese makers of the third class often put his name on their inferior instruments, in order to raise the price of them. Most of the spurious Stainer instruments in the market have this origin. The genuine instruments of this master were formerly classed by Lupot, an excellent maker, of Paris, and by the violinist Cartier, in three periods. To the first belonged the violins dated from Cremona, which have labels written and signed by the hand of Stainer himself; these are of the greatest rarity. They are known by the following characteristics: a small pattern; small and narrow *f* holes; a less elongated scroll than that of the Amati, and larger in front. The wood has a broad grain, and the varnish is like that of Nicholas Amati. A fine instrument of this period passed from M. Desentelles, late Intendant of the King's privy purse, into the hands of Gardel, first Ballet-master at the Opera, and a distinguished amateur of the violin. It bore the date 1644.

So much obscurity hangs over the second period of Stainer, and circumstances are related in such a contradictory manner, that, in the absence of authentic documents, we can only pass it over. All the information that can be gathered from the genuine instruments produced during this period is, that Stainer lived and worked at Absom from 1650 to 1667. It is said that he was then assisted in his labours by his brother, Mark Stainer, who was a monk. A violin which had belonged to the Marquis de la Rosa, a grandee of Spain, and which had been in the hands of Lupot; that of Count de Marp, an amateur of the violin at Paris; another which belonged to Frey, late a member of the opera orchestra, and a music publisher; and lastly, an admirable alto which was in the possession of Matrot de Préville, late governor of the port of Lorient, were formerly the only instruments of the second period of Stainer known as genuine, at Paris. At present, the celebrated violinist, M. Alard, possesses one of the greatest beauty.

According to tradition, Stainer retired to a Benedictine convent, after the death of his wife, and there passed the remainder of his days. It was there that he wished to close his career by the construction of twelve violins of a superior finish, which he sent to the twelve Electors of the Empire. I saw in the hands of Cartier, in 1817, a violin, which had formerly belonged to the Duke of Orleans, grandfather of King Louis Philippe, and had afterwards passed into the possession of the violinist Navoigille, and lastly into that of Cartier: it was said to be one of those twelve precious instruments. The tone—pure, silvery and clear—was charming. The varnish had a beautiful gilded appearance.

There is now, at Paris, a genuine Stainer instrument, which I have heard Sivori play upon, and which, although of a very small pattern, possesses an unusually brilliant and very sympathetic tone. The Count de Castelbarco, of Milan, has likewise an alto of this master, which is a model of perfection as to workmanship, and the tone of which is of extreme beauty. This distinguished amateur possesses two quartetts of Stradivarius, very remarkable instruments; another of Joseph Guarnerius; a fourth of Nicholas Amati; and lastly a quartett of Stainer, of which the alto above-mentioned forms a part.* These instruments, when used for the class of music to which they bear analogy, produce effects which are not obtainable with any others.

From the school of Stainer came Matthias Albani, who was born in 1621 at Botzen or Bolzano, in the Italian Tyrol. Gerber mentions a violin of this artist, which bore on the inside these words: *Matthias Albanus fecit in Tyrol. Bolsani,* 1654. The instruments of this maker have too high an arching: his varnish is of a reddish brown. The third and fourth strings have a nasal sound; the second possesses power and roundness, and the first is brilliant, but dry. Albani died at Botzen in 1673.†

The son of Albani, whose Christian name was also Matthias, was born at Botzen about the middle of the seventeenth century. After learning the art of making

---

* M. Fétis dedicated this work to the late Count de Castelbarco, whose valuable instruments and the original letter of Stradivarius, of which a fac-simile is given herein, were sold on Thursday, June 26th, 1862, by Messrs. Puttick and Simpson. The letter realised the sum of eight pounds.—TR.

† See Moritz Bermann's *Oesterreichische biographisches Lexikon,* Vol. 1. p. 69.

instruments from his father, and labouring in the workshops of Cremona, he made many instruments which have been esteemed nearly equal to those of the Amati. Gerber, who confounds him with his father, mentions two violins by him, which belonged to the violinist and composer Albinoni, one dated 1702, and the other 1709.

There was another Albani who worked in Sicily during the first half of the seventeenth century. His instruments bear no Christian name, and nothing is known of his life. There is, in Brussels, a small violin possessing a brilliant volume of tone, and bearing within the inscription—*Signor Albani in Palermo*, 1633.

Matthias Klotz or Clotz, a Tyrolese maker, was the best pupil of Stainer. After the death of his master, he manufactured instruments, the forms of which are in general imitated from Stainer, but the tone of them has less distinction. Most of the violins of Klotz were made between 1670 and 1696. However, there exist some instruments which bear the name of Matthias Klotz and a later date; but it is thought they were made by the sons of this artist, and that they did not put their own names on the violins and altos which came from their workshops, until after the death of their father.

George, Sebastian and Ægides *(Égide)* Klotz, sons of Matthias, have made violins which are not devoid of merit, but they are less sought for, in Germany, than those of their father. It is said of these artists, that, when an instrument of their make turned out superior to others, and better finished in the details of its form, they had the habit of putting the name of Stainer upon it; to which fraud is attributed the counterfeit Stainers which are found in the market. All the Klotz family lived in the Tyrol, and there formed numerous pupils, the founders of all the manufactories of instruments in that country.

There existed a maker of the name of George Klotz, in 1754, at Mittenwald on the Iser, near Landshut, in Bavaria. I have seen one violin of his, dated from that place, in that year. There is nothing to indicate whether he was the grandson of Matthias.

Among the makers foreign to Italy who had worked under Anthony Stradivarius, we distinguish 1st, Medard, who afterwards worked at Paris, and then at Nancy, from 1680 to 1720. He was the founder of the trade in Lorraine. 2ndly, Ambrose Decombre, of Tournay (Belgium), who, on returning to his own country, worked at his business from 1700 to 1735. He is particularly known for his good basses, which are held in esteem. 3rdly, Francis Lupot, of Stuttgard, who wrought in that city from 1725 to 1750: he was the father of the maker of the same name, who established himself at Paris, in the second half of the eighteenth century. 4thly, and lastly, John Vuillaume, of Mirecourt, who made good instruments from 1700 to 1740.

THE GUARNERI OR GUARNERIUS [FAMILY].

THE Guarneri family, of Cremona, has furnished many distinguished makers of stringed instruments, all of whom have been surpassed by *Joseph*, so justly celebrated for the excellence of his productions. The head of this family, Andrew Guarnerius, born at Cremona, in the first part of the seventeenth century, was one of the first pupils of Nicholas Amati. He worked at his art from 1650 to about 1695. His instruments are estimable for good workmanship in the style of the Amati, although marked by certain peculiar details, by which indeed they are recognised. Their sound is pleasing, but it has little intensity and does not travel far. They are ranked in the market amongst instruments of the second class.

Joseph Guarnerius is generally considered as the eldest son of Andrew, and is said to have been the pupil of his father. He worked from 1690 to 1730. Although he may have been the pupil of Andrew, he has not followed his models. His first tendencies were to assimilate him to Stradivarius, whose contemporary he was; but subsequently he imitated the style of his cousin, named Joseph, like himself, of whom we shall speak presently. He has consequently varied both in his patterns and in the details of manufacture; but his instruments are of good quality and esteemed.

Peter Guarneri, second son of Andrew and brother of the preceding, worked from 1690 to 1725. His first productions are dated from Cremona, but later he established himself at Mantua, where he made a great number of instruments which are not without merit, but which have the fault of too high an arching, and are also wanting in brilliancy.

There was another Peter Guarneri, son of Joseph, and grandson of Andrew. Violins and basses exist of his make, dated from Cremona, from 1725 to 1740. During these fifteen years he produced but few. His instruments resemble those of his father, whose pupil he was, but they have less finish.

It remains for me to speak of the great artist of this family, *Joseph Anthony*, commonly called in Italy *Giuseppe del Jesù*, because many of his violins bear the monogram I$\overset{\dagger}{H}$S upon the label. Up to this time, no positive information has been obtainable of this celebrated maker, so that only vague rumours, more or less romantic, could be gathered concerning his life. He himself had given the most direct indication of his origin, in informing us that he was the nephew of Andrew, by this inscription placed in his instruments: *Joseph Guarnerius Andreæ nepos;* but we had no indication of the date of his birth. Thanks to the persevering researches of M. Vuillaume, an authentic document has been found which dispels all doubt on the last point. It is now proved that Joseph Anthony Guarneri, legitimate son of John Baptist Guarneri and Angela Maria

Locadella, was born at Cremona on the 8th of June, 1683, and was baptized on the 11th of the same month, in the parish of St. Donato, at the chapel of ease of the Cathedral.*

John Baptist Guarneri, father of Joseph *del Jesù*, of whom mention is here made, was the brother of Andrew. It appears beyond doubt that he was a stranger to the manufacture of instruments, for not one is known which is signed with his name. It even seems that his relations with the members of his family were not intimate; for it was neither with Joseph, nor yet with Peter Guarnerius that his son learnt his art, but with Anthony Stradivarius.

Joseph Guarnerius *del Jesù* worked at Cremona from 1725 to 1745. His first attempts were not marked by any characteristic sign of originality, except a certain indifference in the choice of his materials, in the forms—which are variable—and in the varnish. Some years later, we find his instruments made with care: the wood used for the sides and the back is of excellent quality, and cut on the quarter (*sur maille*); the deal of the belly has been well chosen; the varnish, of fine complexion and elastic quality, is of the loveliest tint and rivals that of Stradivarius. The instruments of this period are of small pattern; their outlines are happily designed; the arching, slightly elevated, subsides by a gentle curve to

---

* *Guarneri* (Giuseppe Antonio) figlio de' legittimi conjugl Giovanni Battista Guarneri ed Angela Maria Locadella nacque nella parocchia di San Donato aggregata alla cattedrale il giorno 8 Giugno 1683 e battezato il giorno 11 del detto mese.—Libro di nati dall' 1669 al 1692. G.—Dalla cattedrale di Cremona, li 19 settembre 1855. Signé: *Fusetti Giulio vic°*.

the purfling; the inner parts are formed of good deal. It is only in one respect that criticism is applicable to these instruments, namely, the degrees of thickness, particularly in the middle of the back, are too great; a radical defect, which impairs their elasticity, the freedom of their vibration, and, consequently, the brilliance of their sound. Mounted according to the style of the period when they were constructed, these instruments must have been wanting both in power and in distant transmission of sound. The stamp of originality is apparent in them, notwithstanding the variable forms in which the artist still indulged.

In the third period of his career, Joseph Guarnerius presents a still more surprising variety in the forms of his instruments, while yet preserving that originality and independence of character by which his genius is revealed. During this period, he produced some admirable instruments of a large pattern, made with excellent wood cut on the quarter *(sur maille)*, and conformably to the best conditions possible, in respect to the arching and the degrees of thickness. A beautiful varnish, as remarkable for its fineness and elasticity, as for its color, protects these excellent instruments, which equal in merit the most beautiful productions of Anthony Stradivarius, after being subjected to the alterations made necessary by the requirements of the present time.

All at once, immediately after this glorious period in his career, Guarnerius became so inferior to himself in the instruments which left his hands, that it would be impossible to recognise his productions, if the stamp of originality, which he preserved to the last, in certain details, did not assure us of their being his. Poorness in the wood, in the workmanship, and in the varnish— all strike the eye of a connoisseur in a certain number of [his] violins, the degenerate fruit of a great talent decayed. Such a metamorphosis would be inexplicable, if the unhappy end of this artist, furnished by tradition, did not make known to us the cause of such a great and deplorable change. The reports current in Italy concerning the misfortunes to which Guarnerius was exposed during his latter years are vague and contradictory; but, in comparing them, it certainly appears that the end of this distinguished maker was not that of a good man. Old Bergonzi, who died at Cremona in 1738, at the age of eighty years, and who was grandson of Charles, the pupil of Stradivarius, related that Joseph Guarnerius *del Jesù* had lived an irregular life; that, idle and negligent, he loved wine and pleasure, and that his wife, born in the Tyrol, had not been happy with him, although she had often assisted him in his work. Bergonzi added that Guarnerius had been confined in prison for many years, for some cause now unknown, and that he died there in 1745. Other traditions add some details to these disclosures; for instance, it is said that the gaoler's daughter procured him the woods which he required, some wretched tools, and that she worked with him. It must have been at this unfortunate period that the instruments, so little worthy of the talent of the artist, were produced. This same girl carried about his manufactures and sold them at low prices, in order to procure him some comforts in his misery. She also bought, sometimes from one maker and sometimes from another, the varnish with which he covered his violins; and this explains the reason of the variety of composition and tints which are observable in these productions of a disastrous period.

The reputation of Joseph Guarnerius was not established in Italy until after his death; and it has been much more tardy in France. I remember that, in my youth, while the price of a fine Stradivarius was a *hundred louis* [£100], that of the best Joseph Guarnerius did not exceed *twelve hundred francs* [£48]; but, latterly, their qualities of grand sonority have been recognised, which have caused them to be sought after, and have advanced the price of choice violins to *six thousand francs* [£240]. Among the best violins of this great master, we may place in the first rank that on which Paganini habitually played at his concerts, and which he bequeathed to the city of Genoa, his native place*; that which belonged to the celebrated violinist M. Alard, and one possessed by M. Leduc, an amateur, of Paris; lastly those belonging to Messrs. Goding† and Plowdens, of London.

Some Italian makers have imitated the style of Joseph Guarnerius, particularly Paul Anthony Testore, of Milan, Charles Ferdinand Landolfi, of the same city, and Laurence Storioni, of Cremona; but their productions rank only among instruments of the third class.

---

* An interesting anecdote of this celebrated instrument is related in the charming "History of the Violin and its Professors" by Mr. Dubourg, 4th Edition, p. 359, published by Messrs. Cocks & Co. See also the Appendix to this work.—TR.

† The instruments of the late Mr. Goding were sold in February 1857, by Messrs. Christy and Manson, of King Street, St. James's Square.—TR.

Here ends the history of the manufacture of stringed instruments of the Cremonese school, the phases of which have been so brilliant for nearly two centuries. At the present day, the city of Cremona, whose historic celebrity is due to the labors of certain artists of that profession, no longer offers anything which recalls this ancient splendour of the art. With the exception of some select citizens, the population has not even preserved the remembrance of the Amati, of Stradivarius, or of Guarnerius.

THE BOW

OF

FRANCIS TOURTE.

THE bow, that magic wand, by the aid of which the great artist affects both our heart and our imagination —that talisman which transports us beyond the visible world and causes us to experience the most ineffable delights of the ideal; the bow, like all the inventions of man, originated in feeble essays: its primary elements consisted of light bamboos, or flexible reeds, bent archwise and kept in this position by a hank of hair clumsily fastened at both ends. Thousands of years probably glided away, before a thought occurred of improving this primitive construction.

The first important modifications of the bow seem to belong to Arabia; for we find it depicted, with a fixed nut, among the ornaments of a collection of poems, the manuscript of which, written during the period of the first Caliphs, belonged to Langlès, keeper of the Oriental manuscripts of the National Library of Paris, at the beginning of this century, and, after his death, passed into the Imperial Library of Vienna. I possess a bow of this kind, made at Bagdad, of cherry wood, with a head where the hair is fastened, and a nut fixed in a dovetail notch in the stick.

The figure of a bow-instrument drawn from a manuscript of the ninth century by the Abbot Gerbert, and reproduced in this work, shows an inverse disposition of the bow; for the head has a considerable elevation where the hair proceeds from, which is then carried on and attached to the stick right under the hand of the performer. Bows of the same kind, but larger, are seen in some monuments of the eleventh century; but in the century following, and especially in the thirteenth, considerable ameliorations are introduced in it: we see at this period, in the drawings of some manuscripts, and in certain architectural monuments, bows in which the nut is as high as the head, and which are nearly straight. The bows of the *rebecs* are arcs formed with little care; their construction may enable us to judge of the slight skill of the minstrels who used them.

In the sixteenth century, the bow began to improve; we then see the stick—sometimes round, at others pentagonal—become smaller in approaching the head, which latter is immeasurably elongated. In the following century, the art of playing bow-instruments had improved, and the necessity was felt of modifying the degree of tension of the hair, according to the music which had to be executed; which requirement was met by the invention of the *crémaillère*, a band of metal placed on that part of the stick where the nut is fixed, and divided into a certain number of notches. A moveable loop of iron or brass wire, attached to the nut, served to catch the latter to one of the notches of the *crémaillère*, higher or lower, according to the tension which the performer wished to give to the hair. At this period, the head was always very elongated and ended in a point which turned back a little. The stick was always more or less bent *(bombée)*. Such was the bow of Corelli, and that of Vivaldi. These two masters, who lived at the commencement of the eighteenth century, had not yet experienced the necessity of rendering the stick flexible, because they had no idea of imparting to their music the varied shades of expression [of more modern times]: they were acquainted with but one sort of conventional effect, which consisted in repeating a phrase *piano*, after it had been played *forte*.

It is a remarkable thing, that the construction of bow-instruments had arrived at the highest point of perfection, whilst the bow itself was still relatively in a rudimentary state. Tartini, whose style was more varied than that of Corelli and Vivaldi, about 1730, made some happy ameliorations in this agent, on which depends the production of the sounds. He caused the bows to be made less clumsy, and out of lighter wood than those which had been previously used; he adopted the straight stick, instead of retaining the bent form, shortened the head, and made [small longitudinal] grooves in that part of the stick which is [held] in the hand, so as to prevent its turning between the fingers. The violinist Woldemar, pupil of Mestrino,[*] who became remarkable for his eccentricities at the end of last century

---

[*] Woldemar is stated to have been the pupil of *Lolli*, both on the title-page of his work "*Le nouvel art de l'archet*" and in M. Fétis's *Biographie des Musiciens*, vol. viii, 1844.—Tr.

and in the early years of the present, made a collection of bows of the celebrated ancient violinists of Italy; he gave engravings of those of Corelli, Vivaldi, Tartini, Locatelli and Pugnani, in his *Method for the Violin*, [a work] which met with no success and which is now unfortunately of excessive rarity. It is to be regretted, in this respect, that this indigested work has left the market; for it was not without interest to compare the progressive, though slow, ameliorations of the bow. The result of all the information that can be gathered on this subject is, that no serious attempt was made to improve the bow, until towards the middle of the eighteenth century.

Display of the successive ameliorations of the bows of the seventeenth and eighteenth centuries.

No. 1.—Mersenne, 1620.

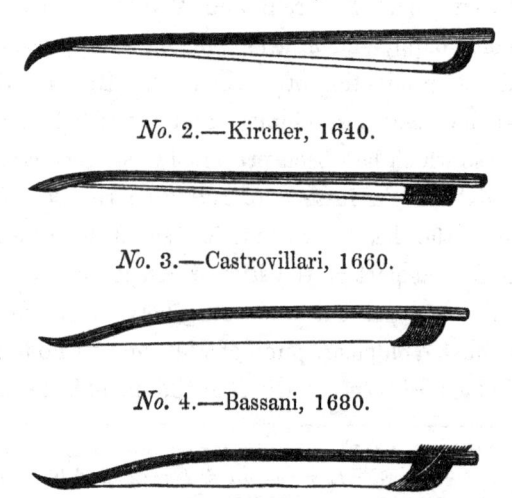

No. 2.—Kircher, 1640.

No. 3.—Castrovillari, 1660.

No. 4.—Bassani, 1680.

No. 5.—Corelli, 1700.

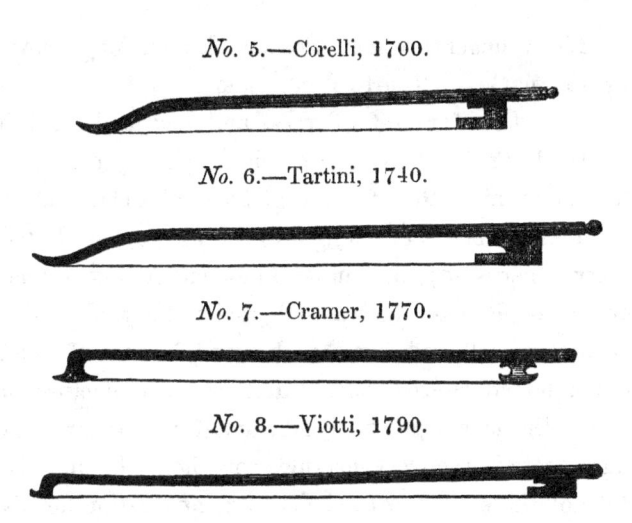

No. 6.—Tartini, 1740.

No. 7.—Cramer, 1770.

No. 8.—Viotti, 1790.

To Tourte, of Paris, the father of him who has carried the bow to its highest perfection, is attributed the suppression of the *crémaillère,* and the substitution of the screw which causes the nut to advance and recede, to tighten the hair at will, by means of a button placed at the extremity of the stick. But, if my memory serves me, I think I have seen representations of bows with buttons, and without *crémaillère,* of a previous period. However that may be, the elder Tourte was a skilful workman: he manufactured bows, fluted very prettily, and improved the heads of them by means of deep mortises which admit of the hanks of hair being fixed in a firmer manner and spread out more equally. About 1775, his eldest son made bows which were then esteemed on account of their lightness; but most of them are constructed with wood of an inferior quality; the sticks are too slender, the heads badly designed, the nuts too narrow and often too high.

His younger brother, Francis Tourte, long known by the name of Tourte Junr., was born in Paris, in 1747, in St. Margaret's Street, and died in the month of April, 1835, at the age of eighty-eight years. Intended by his father for the business of a clockmaker, he entered when very young into a workshop, neglected every other study, and never knew either how to read or write. Perhaps he was indebted to the trade which he at first followed, for the skill and delicacy of hand which he afterwards displayed in the manufacture of bows. Disgusted with his condition, after having passed eight years in the clock-making workshops, because he did not there meet with sufficient remuneration for his needs, he took to the business of his father and brother. At this period, the distinguished artists resident in Paris were making progress towards the art of singing on their instruments, with the shades [of expression] of which the great Italian vocalists had given the example; and they all desired bows which should answer better to the effects which they wished to produce, and which should possess at the same time greater lightness, spring and elasticity. Francis Tourte made his first essays with wood from the staves of sugar-casks, with a view to determine the forms of the bow and to acquire skill in working, without making use of expensive materials. He sold these early products of his manufacture for 20 or 30 sous [10 or 15 pence]. Being an indefatigable investigator, and fully sensible of the important action of the bow in the production of the sounds, he subsequently tried all kinds of wood which appeared to him proper to realise his views; but he was not long in discovering that Fernambuc wood alone would yield the results which he sought to attain, and that it alone combine stiffness with lightness.

The period of the first and important discoveries of Tourte, extends from 1775 to 1780. Unfortunately, the maritime wars of France and England then presented a serious obstacle to the importation of Fernambuc wood on the continent: and the price of this valuable article, used for dying, rose to six francs a pound [about 4s. 9½d.]. Fernambuc wood intended for dying purposes is exported in billets; that which is richest in coloring matter is likewise the best for the manufacture of bows: but it is rare to find billets which are straight and only slightly defective; for this wood is nearly always knotty, cracked inside, and crooked in every direction. Sometimes eight or ten thousand kilogrammes [nearly 8 or 10 tons] of Fernambuc wood scarcely present any pieces with a straight grain and suitable for making good bow-sticks.

The rarity of this wood, at the period here mentioned, explains the enormous price which Tourte asked for his bows: he sold a bow, the nut of which was made of tortoise shell, the head inlaid with mother-of-pearl, and the mounting of the nut and button of gold, for 12 louis (of 24 livres) [£11 4s. 6d.]; his best bows, mounted in silver, with an ebony nut, were sold at 3½ louis [£3 5s. 5¾d.]; and, lastly, ordinary bows, without any ornament, were charged 36 francs [£1 8s. 10d.].

Up to 1775, neither the length nor the weight of bows, nor yet their conditions of equilibrium in the hand had been determined: enlightened by the counsels of celebrated artists, by whom he was surrounded, Tourte fixed the length of the stick of the violin bow, including the button, at 74 or 75 centimètres [29.134 or 29,528 in.]; that of the alto, at 74 centimètres [29.134 in.]; and that of the violoncello at 72 or 73 centimètres [28.347 or 28.740 in.]. At the same time, also, he determined the distance of the hair from the stick by the heights of the head and nut, and obtained by these proportions the angle requisite to the hair for the attack of the strings, avoiding the inconvenience of the latter being touched by the stick. In these bows, the head, more elevated than formerly, and consequently heavier, obliged Tourte perceptibly to increase the weight of the lower part, in order to bring the hand again near the centre of gravity, and to put the bow in perfect equilibrium. It was with this object that he willingly loaded the nut and button with metallic ornaments which augmented the weight of them. Hence it follows that, notwithstanding the lightness of the plain bows, we prefer those which are ornamented, although heavier in appearance; for, in the former, the centre of gravity being removed from the hand, the weight is more perceptible towards the upper end of the stick; while, in the others, it is found in the lower part. In bows which possess the most satisfactory equilibrium, the length of the hair is 65 centimètres [25.59 in.] for the violin, and the centre of gravity is at 19 centimètres [7.48 in.] from the nut; in the violoncello bow, the length of the hair is from 600 to 620 millimètres [23.622 to 24.410 in.], and the centre of gravity is from 175 to 180 millimètres [6.89 to 7.087 in.] from the nut.

M. Vuillaume has seen Tourte himself saw the billets of Fernambuc wood, in order to obtain the straight thread, and that the grain (*maille*) might be placed as it ought to be; he then bent the sticks by means of fire. Some persons have supposed (Norblin was of this number) that Tourte did not bend his bowsticks by fire, but that he cut them out of the billet according to the form which they should have: but this proceeding would have been in manifest contradiction with the principle of the direction of the straight thread, of which he had recognised the excellence. It is therefore certain that he obtained the requisite curvature by heat. He knew that this curvature could not be invariably preserved unless the inside of the stick were heated as well as the outside, in order that all the fibres might concur in maintaining the permanence of the curve. In fact, it has been remarked, that when the sticks are only heated on the outside, the inner fibres, which have not been submitted to the action of the fire, remain in their primitive state and oppose a constant resistance to the direction of the curve; sometimes, even, this resistance is such, that it ends by restoring the stick to its normal condition, particularly when the bow has been exposed to the influence of damp. This is the reason why the bows which are got up apparently cheap lose their curvature and have none of the necessary qualities.

Tourte gave the most scrupulous care to the preparation of the hanks of hair for bows. He preferred the hair of France, because it is larger and stronger than that of other countries. The preparation to which he subjected it consisted in scouring it with soap; he then put it into bran water, and lastly, after removing the heterogeneous particles which had adhered to it, he plunged it into pure water, lightly colored with blue. His daughter was almost constantly occupied in sorting the hairs, rejecting such of them as were not perfectly cylindrical and equal throughout their length: this is a delicate and necessary operation; for not more than one-tenth of a given number of hairs is fit for use, the greater portion having one side flat and presenting numerous inequalities. At the period when Viotti arrived in Paris, the hairs of the bow nearly always clustered together in a round mass, which impaired the quality of the sounds. After making his observations on this point, Tourte conceived the possibility of compelling the hairs to preserve the appearance of a flat plate, like a ribbon, by pinching them at the nut with a ferrule which he at first made of tin, and afterwards of silver. Subsequently, he completed this important amelioration by a little plate of mother-of-pearl, which covered the hair from the beginning of the mortise in the nut to the ferrule by which it is retained. Bows furnished with this plate were called, *archets à recouvrements*.[*] The number of hairs determined on by Tourte for his bows was rather less than has been adopted since players have endeavoured to draw the greatest amount of sound possible from their instruments: this number now varies between 175 and 250, according to the size of the hairs.

---

[*] The little plate or covering over the nut, here described, is called, in England, the *slide*—Tr.

It is in the distribution of forces and the perfection of his sticks that Tourte has shown himself superior to other bow-makers. We naturally inquire, at the present day, how a man destitute of all instruction, and whose education had been neglected to the extent of his being unable either to read or write, could determine, by the mere power of his instinct and the certainty of his eye, the proportions of the progressive diminution of the stick and its swell towards the head. His faculties never failed him, in this respect; as is incontestably proved by the preference accorded to his bows by the most skilful artists over all productions of the same kind, and by the high price which is given for them in the market. Their fame is universal. The difficulty which is experienced in procuring one of them, and the necessity of compensating for them by others which should equal them in quality, have aroused the attention of science, and we have forthwith applied ourselves to the theory of the production of sound by the action of the bow on the strings. Without here entering into all the developments of the researches which have been made, and of the analyses to which this subject has been submitted, I shall remark that learned men have recognised the following fundamental points:

If the continued action of the bow on a string does not stop it from vibrating, whilst the least contact of a finger suffices to check its vibrations, it is because the bow, in passing over it, does not touch it in a continuous manner, but by a succession of very rapid shocks, which are so regular that they keep up the motion instead of destroying it. The regularity of the phenomenon depends on the particular elasticity of the hair, on the action of the particles of rosin with which it is coated, and especially on the ability of the performer's hand. This explains the purpose of the rosin which is rubbed on the hairs of the bow, deprived of which coating the hairs glide over the string without producing any sound: but the roughness occasioned by the rosin deposited on them gives rise to those rapid and regular shocks from whence results the continuity of the vibration.

It is mainly owing to this result that science has been enriched with the theory of the bow; for hitherto she had not furnished the law of the progressive diminution in the size of the stick, found instinctively by Tourte, and so essential to the production of all the phenomena of power, lightness, delicacy and expression by which the artist manifests his talent. We are indebted to M. Vuillaume, of Paris, for the recent discovery of this law, a discovery induced by his intelligent and attentive observations, and of which he has demonstrated the reality by some very ingenious geometrical constructions: the results of which will be appreciated on the perusal of the following analysis, by keeping in view the plate in which these geometrical operations are represented.

EXPERIMENTAL DETERMINATION OF THE FORM OF TOURTE'S BOWS.

The medium length of the bow, to the head exclusively, is $0^m,700$* [27.56 inches, English].

The bow comprises a cylindrical or prismatic part of uniform dimensions, the length of which is $0^m,110$ [4.33 in.]. When this portion is cylindrical, its diameter is $0^m,008\frac{6}{10}$ [.34 in.].

From this cylindrical or prismatic portion, the diameter of the bow decreases up to the head, where it is reduced to $0^m,005\frac{3}{10}$ [.21 in.]; this gives a difference of $0^m,003\frac{3}{10}$ or $\frac{33}{10}$ of a millimètre [.13 in.] between the diameters of the extremities; from whence it follows that the stick comprises ten points where its diameter is necessarily reduced by $\frac{3}{10}$ of a millimètre [.012 in.] reckoning from the cylindrical portion.

After proving by a great number of Tourte's bows that these ten points are not only found always at decreasing distances on the same stick, but also that these distances are perceptibly the same, and that the situations of the points are identical on different bows compared together, M. Vuillaume sought to ascertain whether the positions of these ten points could not be obtained by a geometrical construction, by which

---

* Here, as in the previous parts of this work, the French measurements are given precisely as they stand in the original, and are followed by closely approximating English lengths within brackets.—Tr.

22 mill.

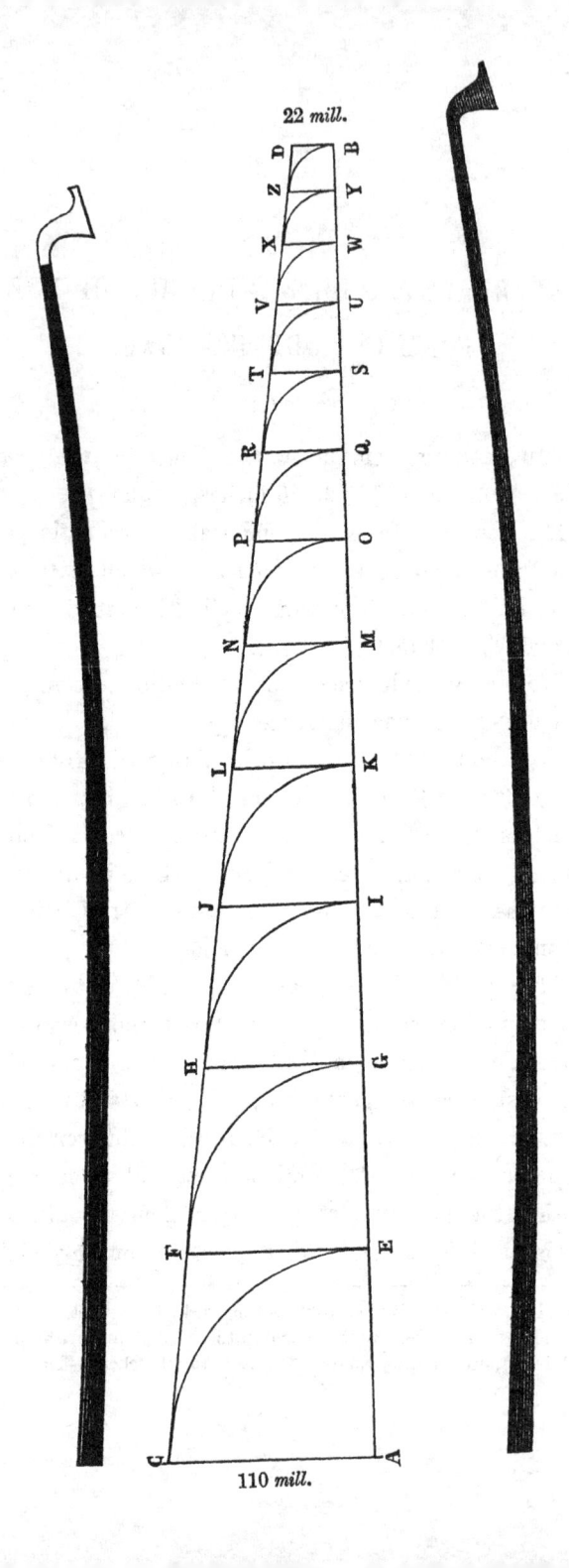

110 mill.

they might be found with certainty; and by which, consequently, bows might be made whose good conditions should be always settled *à priori*. This he attained in the following manner:

At the extremity of a right line A B, equal to $0^m,700$ [27.56 in.], that is to say, the length of the bow, raise a perpendicular A C, equal to the length of the cylindrical portion, namely $0^m,110$ [4.33 in.] At the extremity B of the same line, raise another perpendicular B D, of the length $0^m,022$ [.866 in.] and unite the upper extremities of these two perpendiculars or ordinates by a right line C D, so that the two lines A B and C D may lie at a certain inclination to each other.

Take the length $0^m,110$ [4.33 in.] of the ordinate A C, with the compasses, and set it off on the line A B, from A to E: from the point thus obtained, draw another ordinate (parallel to A C and perpendicular to A B) until it meets the line C D. Between these two ordinates A C and E F—the latter of which is necessarily less than the former—lies the cylindrical portion of the bow, whose diameter, as before stated, is $0^m,008\frac{6}{10}$ [.34in.].

Then take the length of the ordinate last obtained E F and set it off, as before, on the line A B, from F to G, and at the point G draw a third ordinate G H, the length of which must also be set off on the line A B, to determine thereon a new point I, from which draw the fourth ordinate I J; the length of which likewise, when set off on the line A B, determines the point where the fifth ordinate K L is to be drawn. The latter, in like manner, determines the sixth M N, and so of the others, to the last but one Y Z.

The points G I K M O Q S U W Y so obtained, starting from the point E, are those where the diameter of the bow is successively reduced $\frac{3}{10}$ of a millimètre [.012 in.] Now, these points have been determined by the successively decreasing lengths of the ordinates drawn from the same points, and their respective distances progressively decrease from the point E to the point B.

If we subject these data to calculation, we shall find that the profile of the bow is represented by a logarithmic curve of which the ordinates increase in arithmetical progression, while the abscissæ increase in geometric progression; and lastly, that the curvature of the profile will be expressed by the equation:

$$y = -3,11 + 2,57 \log. x;$$

and, in varying x from 175 to 765 tenths of millimètres, the corresponding values of y will be those of the radii [or semidiameters of the transverse circular sections of the bow at corresponding points in the axis].*

In this manner is formulated the rigorous theory of the violin bow. By an analogous geometrical construction, it will be easy to determine the decreasing proportions of the bow of the alto, and of that of the violoncello.

---

* The values of y in tenths of millimètres obtained from the above equation (the ordinates, that is, of the profile of the bow) may be reduced to their equivalents in English inches by multiplying each result by .003937. So also the abscissæ 175 and 765. In entering the table, values of x in English inches may be converted into tenths of millimètres French, by multiplying by 253.99, the reciprocal of the former multiplier—Tr.

FINIS.

APPENDIX,

BY THE EDITOR.

APPENDIX.

No. I.

LETTER OF ANTHONY STRADIVARI, DECIPHERED FROM THE FAC-SIMILE.*

Molto Stim.^{mo} e molto Rev.^{do} mio Sig.^r Padrone Illmo

Compatirà la tardanza del violino, perchè è stato la causa per la vernice per le gran crepate che il sole non le faccia aprire, però V.^a Sig.^a lo riceverà ben aggiustato dentro la sua cassetta e mi spiace che non ho potuto far di più per renderla servita, e per la mia fattura, V.^a Sig.^a mi manderà un Filippo che merita di più ma per servire la di lei persona mi contento. Così qui resto con riverirla di tutto cuore e se valgo in altro la prego delli suoi comandi e le bacio la mano.

Divotissimo Servitore

Di Vostra Molto Illma Sig.^{ia}

ANT.^O STRADIVARI.

Cremona,
  i 2 Agosto 1708.

---

* This task has been accomplished by Signor Manfredo Maggioni, who has also obligingly corrected the translation which follows.—TR.

No. II.

TRANSLATION OF THE PRECEDING LETTER.

Most Esteemed, Very Reverend, and Illustrious Sir,

Pardon the delay of the Violin, occasioned by the varnishing of the large cracks, that the sun may not re-open them. However, you will now receive the instrument well repaired in its case, and I regret that I could not do more to serve you. My charge for the repair will be a Philip.* It should be more, but, for the pleasure of serving you, I am satisfied with that sum. If I can do anything else for you, I beg you will command me; and kissing your hand,

I remain,

Most illustrious Sir,

Your most devoted Servant,

ANTHONY STRADIVARI.

Cremona, August 2, 1708.

---

* *Filippo*—A silver coin then current in Lombardy, of the value of five shillings.

No. III.

SOME ACCOUNT OF PAGANINI'S CELEBRATED GUARNERIUS VIOLIN (MENTIONED AT PAGE 106).

HAVING made enquiry of M. Vuillaume respecting the anecdote of Paganini's violin, as related by Mr. Dubourg, the following was the interesting reply obligingly furnished, with permission to print it in this place:—

TRANSLATION.

In the year 1838, Paganini, on his return from London to Paris, disembarked at Boulogne. He took a coach, in which his violin case, being badly placed, fell, and the concussion was sufficiently violent to unglue one of the inner blocks of the instrument.

On arriving at Paris, Paganini came to me in great distress, his violin having lost its tone. I told him the cause, and said it would be necessary to open the instrument. To this he would not at first consent and manifested extreme anxiety; at length, however, I induced him to allow it to be done, there being no other remedy. He therefore consented, on the express condition that I would do the work myself at his house, and under his own eyes. Although such a delicate operation is more agreeable to accomplish without a looker-on and in the retirement of one's own workshop,

I acceded to his desire, and went to his house for the purpose of taking off the belly of his violin.

It is impossible to describe the torture which Paganini endured during the progress of the work. He twisted about on his chair, made grimaces, and suffered like a martyr; uttering exclamations which plainly showed the affection he entertained for his instrument, and the dreadful fears which he experienced at each crack, caused by the breaking away of the glue, as it yielded to the action of the thin knife used in removing the belly. The task having been accomplished with unexpected success, he entrusted me with this violin, the renown of which was equal to that of its master.

I then resolved to analyse this famous instrument in every part, to take the precise dimensions of it, and to make a similar one. I had some woods of first-rate quality and very old, and could find a back and belly so exactly like those of Paganini's violin, as regards the figure of the maple and the grain of the deal, that I felt assured I should attain a satisfactory result as to quality of tone.

Paganini allowed me three days for the repair of his instrument, and that time sufficed for making mine—at least, the most essential parts of it. I then returned him his violin, with which he was enchanted, and begged me to call again to see it. On proceeding to do so, a few days afterwards, I met him on the Boulevards, when he took my arm and said to me: "I thank you, my dear friend; it is as good as it was before." He then drew from his waistcoat pocket a little red morocco box, saying, "I have had two pins made, the one for the doctor of my body, the other for the doctor of my violin." I opened the little box, and found the pin was ornamented with a capital P. formed with twenty-three diamonds. Astonished at such generosity for so small a labour, and wishing to testify my appreciation of it, I concluded by saying to Paganini I would offer him the violin which I had commenced making like his and on the model of it.

Some months afterwards, I went to his house. He was practising, but, on seeing me enter, he laid his violin on the table. I took mine from its case, and placing it by the side of his, begged that he would accept it. The scene was strange and unaccountable. Paganini became serious and immoveable. A look of doubt and fear overspread his features. Then he seemed surprised. He turned about the violins; changed their places; and, more than once, took the imitation for the original. He was evidently but little pleased to see a violin so similar to his own. At length he seized his bow to try the new violin, and, on sitting down, exclaimed, "It is very good, it is like mine, it has the same tone—the same quality; it is my violin, leave it with me."

Some time afterwards, he came to express his entire satisfaction, and asked me how much I would charge to make him another violin exactly like the former. I replied 500 francs (£20). He then went to Nice, and wrote to me from that place, in the kindest and most friendly manner, enclosing a cheque for the above sum, for another instrument, which I made with the same care as the first, and forwarded to him at Nice; but

Paganini had just expired as the violin arrived there. This instrument is either at Genoa, or at Parma, at the residence of the Baron Achilles Paganini, the son of the illustrious master.

The first of the two violins which I made for Paganini is that on which Sivori plays.

END OF THE APPENDIX.

Advertisement.

VUILLAUME'S
RENOWNED COPIES OF THE OLD MAKERS,
Stradivarius, Guarnerius, the Amatis, Magini, &c.

"Some two thousand or more of M. Vuillaume's instruments have already been sold, and have been, after a little use, preferred, even by good judges, to the genuine old instruments. In these copies the proportions, thicknesses, &c. of the old violins are preserved with scrupulous exactness; the wood (sought out with much labour and at great expense, amongst the weather-beaten châlets of Switzerland) possesses the requisite qualities of age and consequent resonance, and the varnishes have the purity, colour, and fine and limpid appearance of the old Italian varnish."

Price of each Instrument, £14 14s.

Bows.
VUILLAUME'S PATENT BRAZIL-WOOD VIOLIN BOWS,

Ornamented with mother of pearl, gold and silver lapped, and otherwise elegantly finished, with moveable hair, 30s.; without moveable hair, 10s. 6d.

New Hanks of Hair, for Vuillaume's Bows, price 1s. 6d. each.

The Bows of M. Vuillaume's manufacture are remarkable for their perfect balance, and exact division of hair.